Free and Inexpensive
TEACHING TOOLS
To Make and Use

Written by the staff at The Learning Exchange — Denise Chambers, Beverly Clevenger, Pat Cook, Connie Campbell, Janet Fansher, Jenny Isenberg, Pat Loring, Sidney Martin, Sue Mays, Dana McMillan, Laura Mijares-Eubank, Mary Ann Murphree, Elaine Mondschein, Ellen Pittman, and Connie Racer

compiled by Pat Loring

edited by Sidney Martin and Karen Turner

illustrated by Peggy Murray

Cover by Peggy Murray

Copyright © Good Apple, Inc., 1987

GOOD APPLE, INC.
BOX 299
CARTHAGE, IL 62321-0299

ISBN No. 0-86653-388-5

Printing No. 987654321

GOOD APPLE, INC.
BOX 299
CARTHAGE, IL 62321-0299

TABLE OF CONTENTS

Classroom Management

INTRODUCTION

Teaching Tools is designed for use by educators of children from second through sixth grade. The chief materials required for the projects in *Teaching Tools* are containers, such as snack canisters, butter tubs, and egg cartons. All other materials listed for each activity are free or inexpensive items that are easily collected.

Teaching Tools is organized around the basic curriculum areas: language arts, math, social studies, and science. Chapters on bulletin boards and classroom management are included, as well. Each activity in the book affords hands-on experiences for students. Further, each chapter offers ideas that will reinforce basic skills, stimulate research, and inspire creativity.

You may choose to use the ideas as described or to change some of the steps and objectives to better fit your curriculum and your children's needs. Many of the activities are suitable for both remedial and gifted students. In the Bag a Branch activity, for example, some students will observe plant transpiration among several branches, graph the results, and even compare the transpiration rates of different types of trees.

The activities in *Teaching Tools* were developed by the staff at The Learning Exchange, a nonprofit educational resource instruction. During the fifteen years we have served educators in the Kansas City area, we have found that teachers are continually searching for practical classroom activities. In *Teaching Tools* we hope to bring some of the best of our experience to you.

JEREMY   STACY   ALEX   TASHA   JUAN

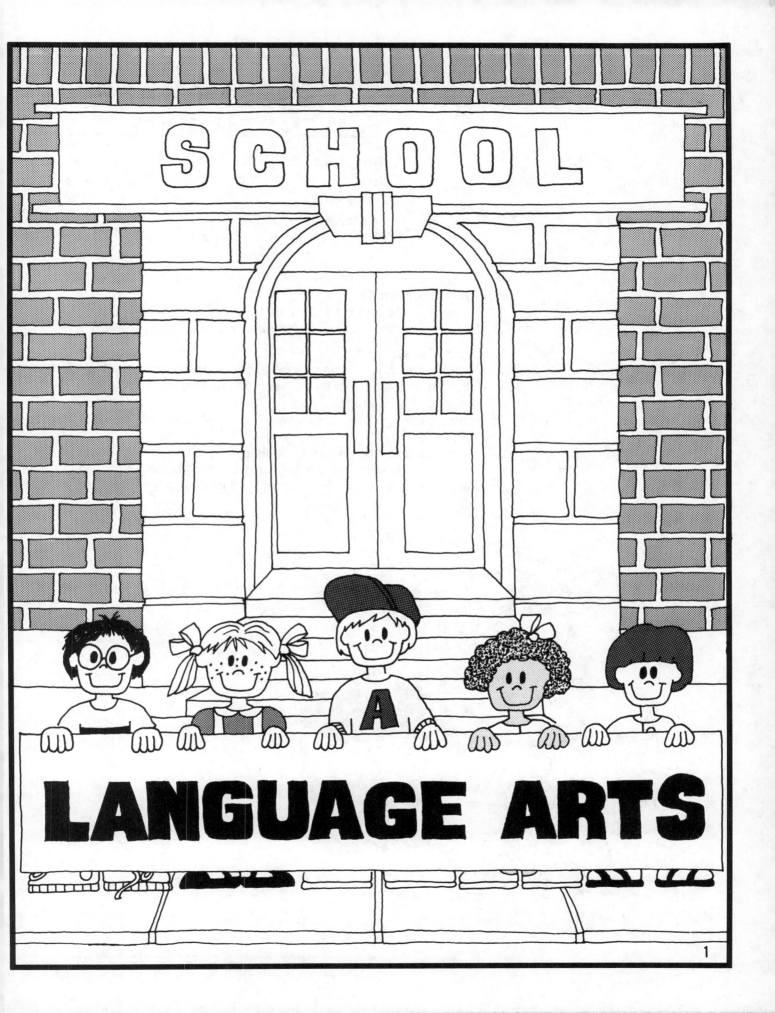

SCHOOL

LANGUAGE ARTS

ABC Containers

Purpose:
Students will practice alphabetizing, naming and comparing.

Materials:
A large variety of containers
Paper
Pencils

Teacher Preparation:
1. Divide the class into three teams.
2. Give each team a set of containers, a piece of paper, and a pencil.

Student Directions:
1. Members of a team work together to choose names for each container in their set. (For example, a box of Cheerios could be a "box," "cereal," or "Cheerios.")
2. After naming the containers, each team lists those names alphabetically.
3. All teams gather to share their lists.
4. Teams check each other's list for proper alphabetizing.
5. Teams compare lists for name similarities; they also observe differences.

LANGUAGE ARTS

Egg Stories

Purpose:
This activity will help students write a creative story.

Materials:
Egg carton
Marble
Paper
Pencil

Teacher Preparation:
1. Select twelve events based on a theme.
   Examples: Hero visits the cave of the dragon.
   Hero goes to see the king.
   Princess screams and then kisses the prince.
2. Write events on small pieces of paper and glue one in each indentation in an egg carton.

Student Directions:
1. Put a marble in the carton, close the lid, and shake.
2. Open the lid; locate the marble. Begin a story about the event shown.
3. When you are ready for another event, shake the egg carton again. Now use the new event in your story. Continue until you are ready to end your story.

Variations:
*Dictate the story into a tape recorder.
*Do the activity as a group project.
*Prepare several egg cartons, each with its own theme.

Build a Burger

Purpose:
Students practice putting words in the correct order to form a sentence.

Materials:
Fast-food hamburger box
Construction paper
Markers
Scissors

Teacher Preparation:
1. Use the patterns and construction paper to make the pictures of the ingredients of a hamburger sandwich.
2. Cut out the pictures.
3. Write one word of a sentence on each pictured ingredient.
4. Number these on the back in the correct order of the sentence.
5. Place all of the ingredients in a fast-food hamburger box.

Student Directions:
1. Open the lid of the hamburger sandwich box.
2. Place all pieces in front of you so that you can see the words.
3. Arrange the words to form a complete sentence.
4. To check your work, turn the ingredients over. If you are correct, the numbers should be in order.

LANGUAGE ARTS

Build a Burger Pattern Page

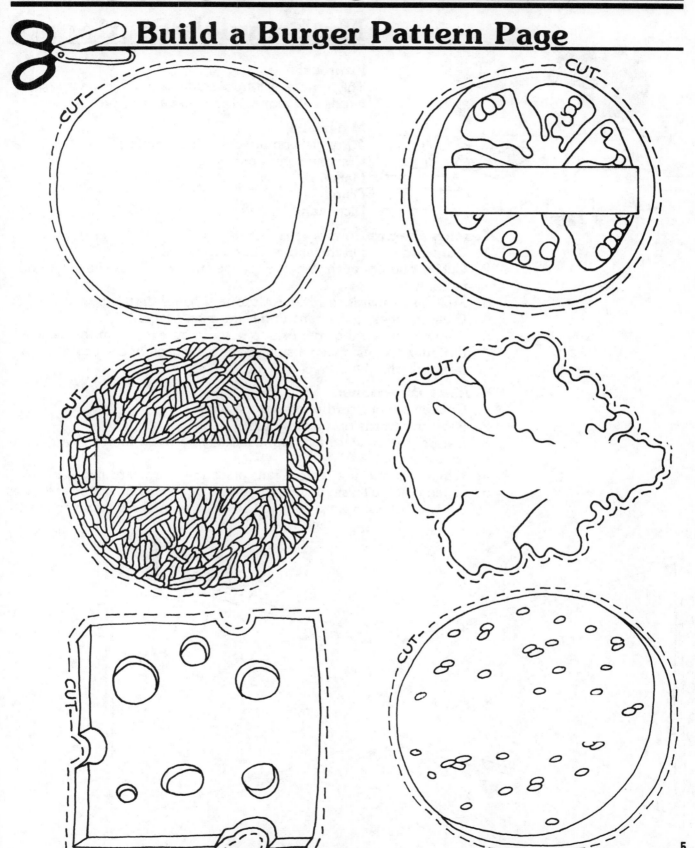

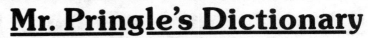

LANGUAGE ARTS

Mr. Pringle's Dictionary

Purpose:
This activity will help students use dictionary guide words and alphabetize vocabulary words.

Materials:
4 Pringle's potato chip cans and lids
Construction paper
Markers
Glue
Dictionary

Teacher Preparation:
1. Cut word cards in the shape of potato chips.
2. Cut bow ties for each Pringle's can (see pattern). Make each tie a different color.
3. Print guide words from four dictionary pages on the bow ties.
4. Glue bow ties to the cans under the man's face.
5. Prepare the word cards. Print one word on each from the selected dictionary pages. Make a small dot on the back of each card to correspond with the correct bow tie.

Student Directions:
1. Choose a word card and read the word.
2. Read the words on the bow ties.
3. Decide if your word falls alphabetically between the two words on each bow tie.
4. When you find the correct can, place the word card inside it.
5. When you are finished, check your answer by matching the color on the back of your word card to the color of the bow tie on the can.

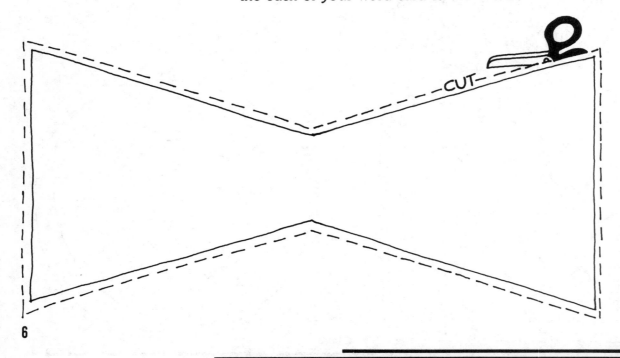

CUT

LANGUAGE ARTS

Syllable Clip

Purpose:
Students will identify words and count syllables.

Materials:
12″ pizza wheel
12 spring clothespins
Marker

Teacher Preparation:
1. Divide the wheel into 12 pie-shaped sections. In each section, write a word of more than one syllable.
2. On the other side of the wheel, mark in dots the number of syllables each word contains.
3. Mark each clothespin with dots that represent the syllables in the words you have chosen.

Student Directions:
1. Choose a word on the pizza wheel.
2. Decide how many syllables the word has.
3. Find a clip with the same number of dots and clip it on the wheel next to your word.
4. Do the same thing for the other words.
5. Check your answer by looking on the back of the wheel.

Variations:
*Do this activity as a group. Ask students to take turns and check

LANGUAGE ARTS

Spin-a-Tale

Purpose:
Students practice expressing their ideas in story form and writing imaginatively.

Materials:
1 brad
9″ pizza wheel
14″ pizza wheel
Marker
Pencil
Paper

Teacher Preparation:
1. Center the small wheel on the large wheel and fasten together with the brad.
2. Mark both circles into six equal pie-shaped sections.
3. On the inside wheel, write the names of characters or people whom students would enjoy writing about.
4. On the outside wheel write situations such as:
   "In outer space with . . ." or
   "On a deserted island with . . . ."

Student Directions:
1. Choose a character from the inside wheel.
2. To match your character with a situation, spin the inside wheel.
3. Write or tell a short story about the character and the situation.

Variation:
*Substitute types of writing for the situations.

Examples: humor
fiction
biography
poetry

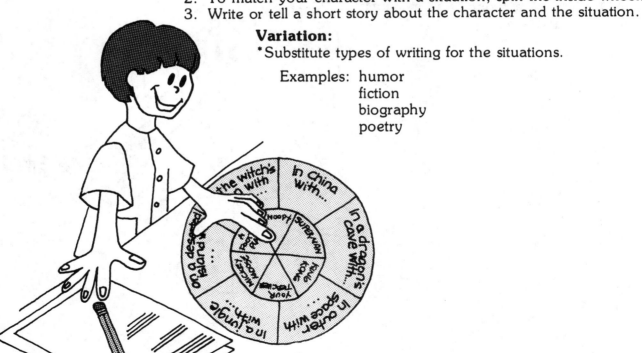

LANGUAGE ARTS

Can It

Purpose:
Students will practice alphabetizing.

Materials:
Cans or containers with lids and labels
Paper
Marker
Small cards

Teacher Preparation:
1. Print the ingredients from each label on individual cards that will fit into the cans or containers.
2. On separate cards or on the lids, list the ingredients in alphabetical order.

Student Directions:
1. Pour the cards from one can.
2. Read each card.
3. Put the cards in alphabetical order.
4. Check your answers.

Variations:
*For lower level students, choose only basic ingredients. For higher level students, print the contents exactly as they appear on the label.

LANGAUGE ARTS
Pop Go the Words

Purpose:
This activity will help students match antonyms (opposites).

Materials:
Popcorn box
Construction paper
Marker
Scissors

Teacher Preparation:
1. Cut 16 to 20 popcorn-shaped word cards out of construction paper (see pattern).
2. Prepare a list of antonyms. Example: above, below; narrow, wide; alike, different; always, never.
3. Print one word on each card.
4. Print game directions on the popcorn box.

Student Directions:
1. Read the popcorn word cards.
2. Match the antonyms and place pairs in front of you.

Variations:
*Make this game self-checking by color coding the backs of the word cards.
*Use the same activity to match synonyms, basic math facts, or science facts.

LANGUAGE ARTS

Poetry in Motion

Purpose:
Students will choose verbs and use them in creative poetry.

Materials:
2 potato chip cans
12 word cards that fit inside the cans
2 markers
Paper

Teacher Preparation:
Display the materials.

Student Directions:
1. Choose a partner.
2. Each partner takes six cards and prints an action word (verb) on each.
3. Exchange cards.
4. Read the words.
5. Write a poem using all six of the action words.
6. Read your poem to your partner.
7. Store the cards in the potato chip container.

Variations:
*Students use their own verbs to write their poems.

*Teacher provides the verbs.

LANGUAGE ARTS
Stump Your Friend

Purpose:
This activity will help students build their vocabularies, and strengthen their spelling and dictionary skills.

Materials:
1 gallon milk jug
A large supply of cards
Dictionaries
Pencils

Teacher Preparation:
1. Cut an opening in the milk carton large enough for the cards and a child's hand.
2. Label the container with the title of the game.
3. Give each student two cards.

Student Directions:
1. Think of the hardest word you know.
2. Look it up in the dictionary.
3. Print the word, pronunciation, and definition on one of the cards. Keep this card.
4. Print the word on the other card; place this card inside the milk carton.
5. To play the game, draw a card from the jug. (If you pick your own card, draw again.)
6. Pronounce the word and give the definition.
7. The person who wrote the card tells whether the word was pronounced and defined correctly.
8. Call on someone else to spell the word. Is the spelling correct?
9. The speller draws a new card from the milk carton.

Variations:
*Try to "stump your teacher" with this game.
*Have students make three cards for each word.
> 1. Spelling
> 2. Pronunciation
> 3. Definition
>
> Play a game similar to Rummy by trying to collect sets of three matching cards.

LANGUAGE ARTS

Cut-Up Comics

Purpose:
Students will practice sequencing with comic strip pictures.

Materials:
5 fast-food French fry boxes
5 brads
5 Sunday newspaper comic strips
1 long strip of cardboard
Hole punch
Laminator or clear plastic
Scissors
Paper
Glue

Teacher Preparation:
1. Laminate the comic strips or cover with clear plastic paper.
2. Cut the comic panels apart.
3. Print five labels naming each comic strip.
4. Glue the labels on the French fry box.
5. Punch a hole in the back of each box.
6. Using the brads, attach each box to the strip of cardboard.
7. Place the cut-up comics in the correct boxes.

Student Directions:
1. Take out all of the pieces from one box.
2. Arrange the panels of the comic strip in the correct order.

Variations:
*Ask students to prepare the activity themselves.
*Make the exercise self-checking by numbering the panels on the back.

Spellbinding Doughnuts

Purpose:
This activity will help students study their spelling words.

Materials:
A doughnut box for each child
Construction paper
Markers

Teacher Preparation:
1. Give each child a doughnut box to decorate.
2. Make a large supply of construction paper doughnuts.

Student Directions:
1. Decorate your doughnut box.
2. Each week, print your spelling words on the paper doughnuts.
3. Put your spelling words in the doughnut box to take home to study.
4. On the back of each paper doughnut, write a sentence using your spelling word.
5. After your spelling test, decorate each doughnut.

Variations:
*Alphabetize the paper doughnuts.
*Keep each week's doughnuts for review.
*Personalize the spelling list so each child has a different set of spelling words.
*Take a field trip to a doughnut shop.
*Make doughnuts as a class project.

LANGUAGE ARTS

Stitch-a-Sentence

Purpose:
Students will practice putting words in proper sequence.

Materials:
Styrofoam meat tray
Yarn 2' to 4' in length
Paper clip
Marker
Small plastic ring

Teacher Preparation:
1. Make up a complete sentence.
2. Write the words in random order on a styrofoam meat tray.
3. Poke a hole through the styrofoam near each word.
4. Make a "needle" by straightening one end of the paper clip and bending the other end to form an "eye."
5. Tie one end of the yarn through the eye. Tie the other end to the plastic ring, which serves as a knot.

Student Directions:
1. Read the words.
2. Sew the words together to form a sentence.

Variations:
*Sew letters in alphabetical order.
*Stitch math equations together by ordering sums from smallest to largest.
  Example: 3 + 9, 8 + 5, 5 + 9, 7 + 8

LANGUAGE ARTS
Name Game

Purpose:
Students will practice writing rhyming words and poems.

Materials:
A variety of containers
Pencils
Paper

Teacher Preparation:
Display the materials.

Student Directions:
1. Look at each container.
2. Print the word for the container and at least one word that rhymes with it.
   Example: jar, car, far, star
              cup, pup, up
              sack, back, rack, jack, smack
3. Do this for each container.
4. Choose one container and use your rhyming words to write a poem.

LANGUAGE ARTS

Dress Your Address

Purpose:
Students will practice addressing envelopes and mailing them.

Materials:
A large number of envelopes
Pencils
Construction paper
Marker
2 shoe boxes
Glue

Teacher Preparation:
1. Decorate the boxes to look like mailboxes.
2. Label the boxes "In Town" and "Out of Town."
3. Prepare a list of addresses that need to be capitalized, punctuated, etc.
4. Print corrected addresses on an answer key.

Student Directions:
1. Choose an envelope.
2. Print one of the addresses on an envelope. Correct it as you write it down.
3. Use the answer key to check your work.
4. When you have addressed the envelope correctly, place it in the right mailbox.

Variations:
*Place the incorrect addresses in a pile. Have student teams draw from the pile and decide what corrections are needed.

*Write a letter to a family member or friend. Address the envelope and mail the letter at the post office.

Bag-a-Story

Purpose:
Students will practice creative writing.

Materials:
6 different containers
      Examples: strawberry container
                     tuna can
                     sack
                     hamburger box
                     pill bottle
                     egg carton
Paper
Pencils

Teacher Preparation:
1. Line up the containers on a table.
2. Print an opening sentence or story starter on the chalkboard.

Student Directions:
1. The six containers you see will help you write a six-part story.
2. Read the opening sentence on the chalkboard.
3. Look at the first container. Continue the story by using that container as an idea for part of the story.
4. Use the rest of the containers the same way, concluding your story with an idea about the last container.

Variations:
*Arrange the containers in a different order.
*Write group stories using the same materials.

"The detective was surprised when he went to the scene of the crime."

LANGUAGE ARTS

Soapbox Speaking

Purpose:
Students build a podium for use in public speaking.

Materials:
Extra large detergent box
1 piece of stiff cardboard
Tape
Wrapping paper (optional)
Strong scissors or knife

Teacher Preparation:
Display the materials and follow the procedure for construction.

Student Directions:
1. Cut the detergent box as shown in the diagram.
2. Wrap the box with paper, if desired.
3. Tape the rectangular shaped piece of leftover detergent box to cover the hole (see diagram).
4. Place the stiff piece of cardboard on the detergent box.
5. Cut out a narrow place in the bottom of the detergent box (see diagram).
6. Place a book in the narrow space for weight and balance.

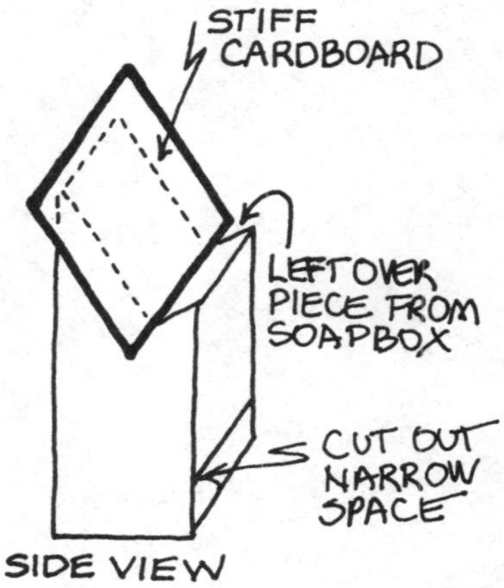

STIFF CARDBOARD

LEFTOVER PIECE FROM SOAPBOX

CUT OUT NARROW SPACE

SIDE VIEW

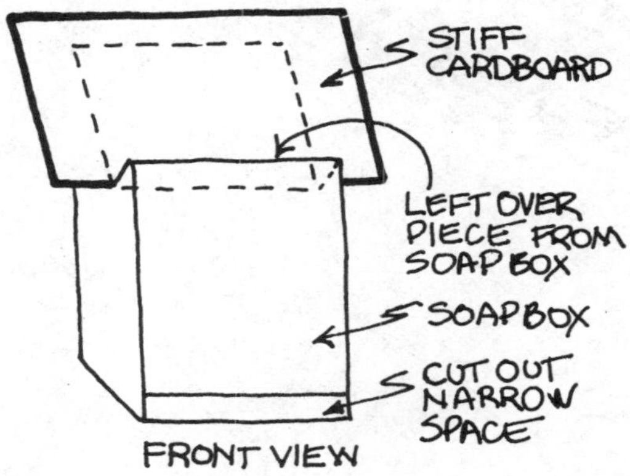

STIFF CARDBOARD

LEFT OVER PIECE FROM SOAP BOX

SOAPBOX

CUT OUT NARROW SPACE

FRONT VIEW

Roll-Over Story

Purpose:
Students will read parts of a story and practice putting them in proper sequence.

Materials:
Printed cereal box (front cover only)
Scissors
Marker

Teacher Preparation:
1. Print a story on the back of a cereal box cover.
2. Cut out each sentence in a horizontal strip.
3. Scramble the sentence strips.

Student Directions:
1. Read the sentence.
2. Place the sentences in order from top to bottom.
3. Check yourself by flipping over each strip as if opening a book. If you are correct, the picture on the cereal box cover will be in the correct order.

LANGUAGE ARTS

Promote the Product

Purpose:
Students will create a new product and design a promotion.

Materials:
A variety of containers
Construction paper
Glue
Markers
Pencil
Paper

Teacher Preparation:
Display the materials.

Student Directions:
1. Choose a container.
2. Think of a new product for that container.
3. Use construction paper and markers to design a label.
4. Glue the new label on the container.
5. Write a promotional paragraph selling the new product and describing its use.

Variations:
*Write a jingle or poem to tell about the new
 product.
*Tape-record the promotions for use as radio
 commercials.
*Videotape the students' promotions for
 use as TV commercials.

LANGUAGE ARTS
Catalog the Carton

Purpose:
This activity will help students read for comprehension, analyze material, and categorize information.

Materials:
Containers with information-filled labels
    Example: cereal boxes
                soup cans
Paper
Marker
Pencils

Teacher Preparation:
1. Print the directions.
2. Display the materials.

Student Directions:
1. Read the information on the container.
2. Make a list of different categories of information found on the label.
   Example: recipes
            contents
3. Tell how the types of information are different or similar.
4. Tell why this information is on the package.
5. List any selling points emphasized on the package.

Variation:
*Contrast types of information listed on several different containers.

22

MATH

MATH
Double Up

Purpose:
Students will double quantities in a recipe.

Materials:
Food containers with recipes printed on the labels
Index cards
Pencils

Teacher Preparation:
Display the materials.

Student Directions:
1. Choose a container.
2. Read the recipe on the container.
3. Double the recipe and record the new recipe on an index card.
4. Write how many people your new recipe will serve.

Variations:
*Triple the recipe or divide it in half.

*Research the cost of the recipe by using newspaper advertisements or visiting a grocery store.

MATH
Measure It

Purpose:
Students will compare standard and metric capacity measurements.

Materials:
Standard measuring cup
Liter container
Water
Funnel
Task cards
Pencil
Paper
Metric and standard measuring charts

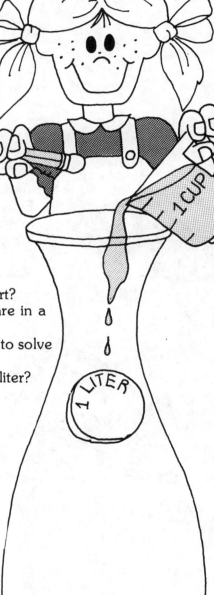

Teacher Preparation:
1. Display the charts at a center.
2. Provide the materials for students.
3. Prepare task cards.
   Examples:
   1. Measure the pints in a liter.
      How many pints are in a quart, according to the chart?
      Use this information to figure out how many quarts are in a liter.
   2. How many cups are in a liter? What is the easiest way to solve the problem?
   3. What is a dekaliter? How many gallons are in a dekaliter? Write how you found your answer.

Student Directions:
1. Read the task card.
2. Use any of the available materials to solve the problem.
3. Write your answer on the paper.

Variation:
*Have students work in small groups or teams.

25

MATH
Cans and Wires

Purpose:
Students will estimate container circumferences, compare relationships of circumferences to straight lines, and graph the results.

Materials:
Round containers in a variety of sizes
Thin wire
Yardstick or meter stick
Wire cutters

Teacher Preparation:
Display the materials.

Student Directions:
1. Estimate the circumference of each container in inches or centimeters.
2. Wrap wire around each container.
3. Cut the wire.
4. Measure each wire.
5. Graph the containers and wires from largest to smallest.

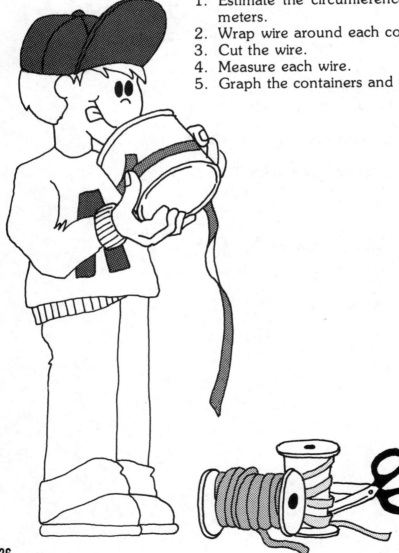

MATH

MATH

Sweet Solutions

Purpose:
Students will determine which math process is necessary to solve word problems.

Materials:
4 doughnut boxes
Construction paper
Scissors
Marker

Teacher Preparation:
1. Label each box with a different math sign ($+$, $-$, $\times$, or $\div$).
2. Cut several doughnuts from construction paper.
3. Write a word problem on each doughnut.

Student Directions:
1. Read each problem.
2. Decide what you would have to do to solve the problem (add, subtract, multiply, or divide).
3. Place the doughnut into the correct box.

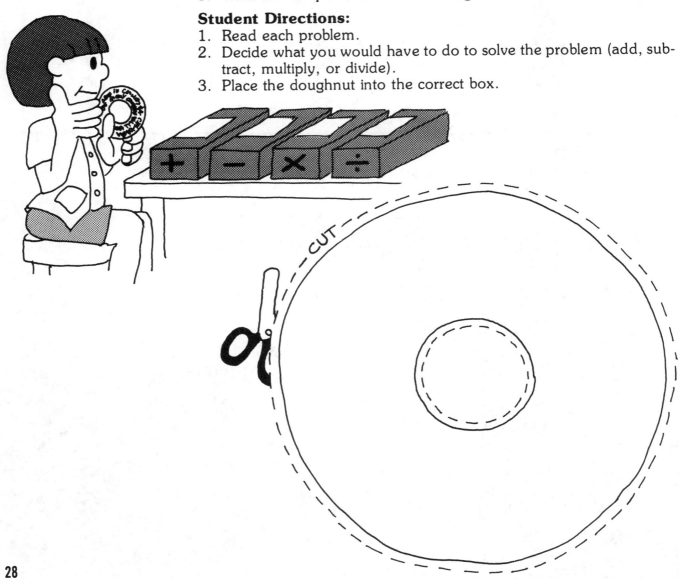

MATH

Chip In

Purpose:
Students will review basic multiplication facts.

Materials:
6-10 film cans with lids
30 round plastic chips
Permanent marker
Colored tape
Large butter tub with lid

Teacher Preparation:
1. Put a small piece of tape on the side of each film can.
2. Write a different numeral on the tape on each can. The numbers should be the products of multiplication facts.
3. Write a multiplication problem on each plastic chip. Make several chips for each can (Examples: 4 x 5, 1 x 20, and 2 x 10).
4. Store all of the materials in the butter tub.
5. Print the game directions on the lid of the butter tub.

Student Directions:
1. Line up the film cans in front of you.
2. Read the problem on each plastic chip.
3. Place the chip into the correct film can.
4. When you are finished, put the lids on the film cans and ask a friend to check your answers.

Variation:
*Use the same procedure to practice addition, subtraction, or division problems.

MATH
Egg-zactly

Purpose:
Students will study sets to develop the concept of multiplication.

Materials:
Egg cartons
Beans (or small chips)
Paper
Margarine container
Pencils

Teacher Preparation:
1. Print a work sheet for the students. Make copies.
   Examples: 1. Count out four beans into each egg cup.
   2. How many beans are there in 3 cups? (3 x 4)
   3. How many beans are there in 6 cups? (6 x 4)
2. Store the beans in the margarine container.

Student Directions:
1. Follow the directions on the work sheet.
2. Use the beans and egg cups to find the answers.
3. Write your answer beside each question.

Variation:
*Write questions on index cards with the correct answers on the back sides for self-checking.

MATH

Guess What?

Purpose:
Students will practice estimation.

Materials:
1 clear plastic milk jug or large jar, with lid
A large supply of cheese balls
1 piece of paper
Pencils

Teacher Preparation:
1. Fill the container with cheese balls, counting as you go. Put on the lid.
2. Place the filled container at a center.
3. Hang the paper by the center and provide pencils.

Student Directions:
1. Look at the container.
2. Guess how many cheese balls are in the jar.
3. Write your answer on the paper.
4. Be sure to put your name by your guess.
5. The person closest to the correct number will help the class share the cheese balls.

Variations:
*Fill the container with a different set of objects each week.

*Graph the guesses to see whether students can improve their estimation skills.

*Put a student in charge of counting the objects and filling the container.

*Try filling different-sized containers.

31

MATH
Milk Carton Computer

Purpose:
Students will review basic facts and check their own answers.

Materials:
Half-gallon milk carton
Lightweight cardboard
Small box
15-20 cards
Con-Tact paper
Masking tape
Marker

Teacher Preparation:
1. On one side of the milk carton, cut two rectangles, one 3½" above the other, large enough for a card to go through.
2. Tape the lightweight cardboard inside the milk carton from the top of the upper slot to the bottom of the lower slot.
3. Tape the small box to the other side of the milk carton so that the flash cards can be stored there.
4. Tape the top of the milk carton shut.
5. Cover the carton with Con-Tact paper.
6. Make a set of basic fact cards, with problems on one side and answers on the other.
7. Cards are inserted problem-side up into the top slot. The curve of the cardboard will reverse the card so that it emerges answer-side up from the bottom slot.

Student Directions:
1. Read the problem on the flash card.
2. Say the answer.
3. Check yourself by inserting the card problem-side up into the top slot. The card will come out of the bottom slot answer-side up.

Variation:
*Make cards to review several skill and curriculum areas:

    Fractions
    Place values
    States and capitals
    Word skills
    Animal facts

MATH

Milk Carton Computer Assembly Page

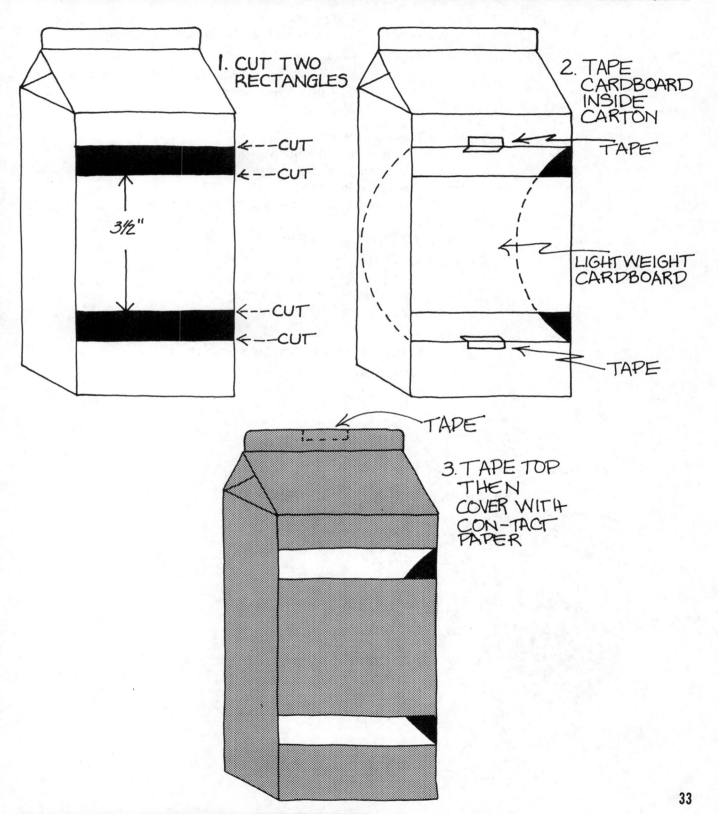

1. CUT TWO RECTANGLES

←--CUT
←--CUT

3½"

←--CUT
←--CUT

2. TAPE CARDBOARD INSIDE CARTON

TAPE

LIGHTWEIGHT CARDBOARD

TAPE

TAPE

3. TAPE TOP THEN COVER WITH CON-TACT PAPER

MATH
Cheeseburger Check

Purpose:
Students will reinforce basic math skills.

Materials:
Fast-food double-sized sandwich container
Construction paper
Marker

Teacher Preparation:
1. Use the pattern to make problem cards.
2. Print a problem and an answer on each problem card. Some of them should be incorrect.
3. Print *right* in one section of the container and *wrong* in the other section.
4. Store the problem cards inside the container.

Student Directions:
1. Read each problem and each answer.
2. Decide whether the answer is right or wrong.
3. Place the card into the correct section.

Variations:
*Have the students make their own problem cards.
*Students may correct the problems.

Cheeseburger Check Pattern Page

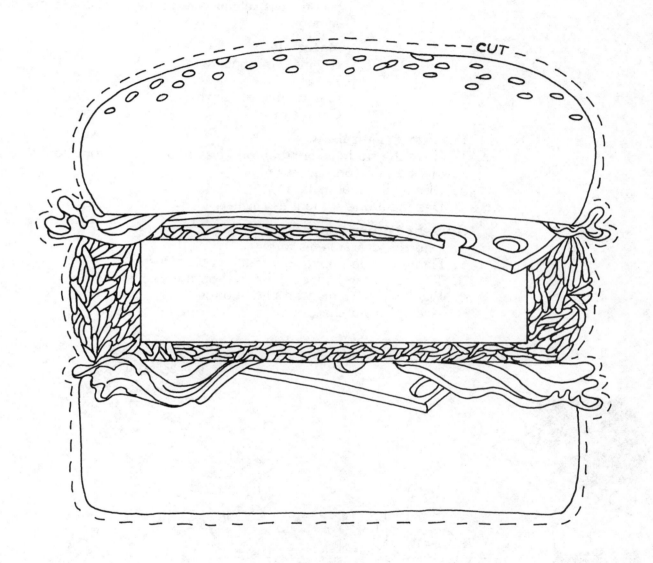

CUT

MATH
Grocery Math

Purpose:
Students will use addition, subtraction, and multiplication skills, along with money skills, in a practical setting.

Materials:
A variety of containers
Paper
Play money or chips
Calculator

Teacher Preparation:
1. Have the students bring empty, clean containers from home.
2. Mark a price on each item.
3. Display the materials.
4. Designate one student as *cashier*.

Student Directions:
1. Choose several items to buy.
2. Figure out on paper how much you have spent.
3. The cashier will check your total on the calculator.
4. Pay for your items with play money.
5. After your purchase, you may become the cashier.

MATH

What a Place

Purpose:
Students will study place value by doing addition problems with regrouping.

Materials:
Half of an egg carton with lid attached
Plastic dots or chips in two colors, such as red and white
Markers
Paper
Pencil
Butter tub

Teacher Preparation:
1. Using the marker, prepare the egg carton as shown in the diagram.
2. Place 20 chips of each color of chips into the butter tub.
3. Print a problem on the inside of the egg carton lid.
   Example: 25
             +46

Student Directions:
1. Read the problem inside the egg carton.
2. Look at the first number (25). Place 2 red chips in the upper left cup for the 2 tens and 5 white chips in the upper right cup for the 5 ones.
3. Follow the same procedure for the next number (46) in the middle pair of cups.
4. Place the white chips from both cups in the lower right cup.
5. Place the red chips from both cups in the lower left cup.
6. How many white chips are there? If there are 10 or more, trade 10 white chips for 1 red chip from the butter tub.
7. Place the red chip in the lower left cup.
8. Now count the red chips in the lower left cup. Count the white chips in the lower right cup.
9. Record the problem and your answer.

Variations:
*Prepare several egg carton problems to solve.

*Ask the students these questions:
 When will the chips NOT need to be traded?
 When will there not be enough cups in the egg carton?

MATH
Ounces of Fun

Purpose:
Students will review standard measurement of volume.

Materials:
Tagboard
Markers
Game pawns
Spinner
Milk containers (gallon, half-gallon, quart, pint, and half-pint)
A dry ingredient, such as rice

Teacher Preparation:
1. Prepare a gameboard similar to the one shown on the next page.
2. Label each container with its volume.
3. Prepare game cards with questions.
   Examples: How many pints are in a quart?
   How many pints are in a half-gallon?
4. Display the materials at a center.

Student Directions:
1. Choose a playing piece and place it in the Start circle.
2. The first player draws a card and answers the question. Use the milk containers and rice to help you figure out the answer.
3. Spin the spinner to see how far you will move along the gameboard.
4. Players take turns until one player reaches Finish.

MATH

Ounces of Fun Gameboard

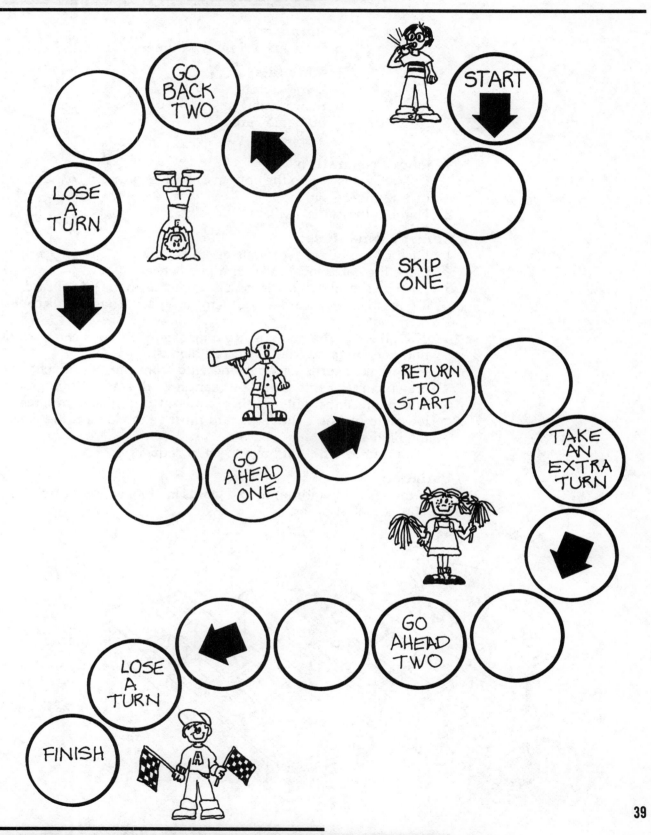

MATH
Calculating Carton

Purpose:
Students will review numerical order.

Materials:
2 egg cartons
Sharp knife
50 game cards
Marker

Teacher Preparation:
1. Cut five thin slits into the bottom of each egg carton so that one card can fit in each slit.
2. Number the cards 1-50.

Student Directions:
1. Each of the two players gets an egg carton.
2. Place the cards face down in a pile between you.
3. Each player takes 5 cards, one at a time, from the pile of cards. Card 1 goes into slit 1, card 2 goes into slit 2, etc. These cards cannot be rearranged.
4. The object of the game is to replace cards in your carton until the numbers progress from lowest to highest.
5. Players take turns drawing one card from the pile. Exchange the drawn card for one from your carton or discard it, if you choose.
6. The game ends when all five cards of one player progress from lowest to highest. The front card must be the lowest, the back card the highest.
(The numbers do not have to be in sequential order.)

Variation:
*Use the same idea for arranging words in alphabetical order or events in chronological order.

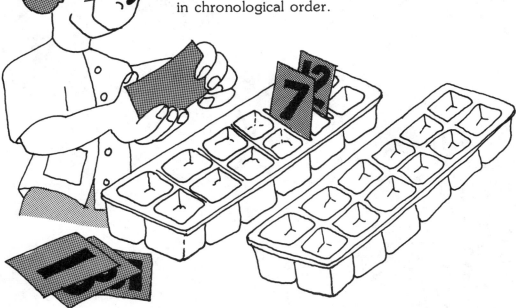

40

MATH
Sewing Solutions

Purpose:
Students will match basic math facts with answers.

Materials:
Styrofoam meat tray
Yarn
Brads
Marker
Scissors

Teacher Preparation:
1. On the left side of the meat tray, write a series of basic math problems.
2. On the right side of the tray, write the answers to the problems at random.
3. Poke a hole beside each problem and each answer.
4. Cut the yarn into lengths or pieces.
5. Tie each yarn length or piece to a brad. Fasten a brad in the hole beside each problem.

Student Directions:
1. Solve each problem.
2. Find the answer on the right side of the tray.
3. Sew the yarn from the problem to the correct answer. Poke the yarn end into the hole beside the answer.

Variation:
*Match any pairs of facts:
    Parts of speech with examples
    States with capitals
    Historical events with dates
    Foods with food groups

MATH
Around and Around

Purpose:
Students will explore and experiment with circles.

Materials:
A variety of round container lids
Construction paper
Scissors
Markers
Pencils

Teacher Preparation:
1. Display the materials at a center.
2. Print the student directions on construction paper as a sign for the center.

Student Directions:
1. Trace a lid onto construction paper. Cut out the circle.
2. Try cutting a circle without a pattern. Compare the two circles.
3. Cut a square. Now use the square to cut a circle. Try it with a triangle and a rectangle.
4. Write down the steps for cutting a circle from a square. See if a friend can follow your directions.
5. Try to invent a new way to cut a circle. Share your idea.

MATH

Measuring Mania

Purpose:
Students will practice their measuring skills.

Materials:
5 large boxes
5 identical sets of containers
    Example of one set: juice can, soup can, small
                            box, film can, cereal box,
                            coffee can, tuna can

Paper
Pencils

Teacher Preparation:
1. Fill each large box with one set of containers.
2. Make up a work sheet with measuring challenges related to the containers in the boxes.
    Example: radius of #1
                cubic inches of #2
                perimeter of #3
                depth of #4
                area of #5
                circumference of #6
                Draw a circle around container #7. Divide the circle into
                six equal slices. How many degrees are in each angle?
3. Number each container to correspond with a challenge.
4. Divide the class into five teams.

Student Directions:
1. Each team should have a large box of containers, a work sheet, and a pencil.
2. Read the work sheet and solve the challenges together.
3. Read your answers to the teacher. If an answer is incorrect, try again.
4. The winning team will answer all of the challenges correctly. It may not be the fastest team. All teams could win.

Variation:
*List all of the tools you used to solve the
                            challenges.

MATH

Where the Chips Fall

Purpose:
Students will review numerical order, using greater than and less than symbols.

Materials:
Egg carton
1 plastic chip
Marker
Pencil
Paper

Teacher Preparation:
1. Print one numeral on the outside lid of the egg carton.
2. In each egg cup inside the carton, print a different numeral.
3. Place the chip inside the carton.
4. Place all of the materials at a center.

Student Directions:
1. Look at the numeral on the egg carton lid.
2. Shake the carton.
3. Open it up. Look at the number where the chip fell.
4. Is that number greater than or less than the numeral on the carton lid?
5. Record your answer on the paper, using the correct sign.
6. Continue playing until you have recorded six different answers.

Variation:
*Provide several cartons for further practice.

TASHA
25 > 10
25 < 36
25 > 23

>25<

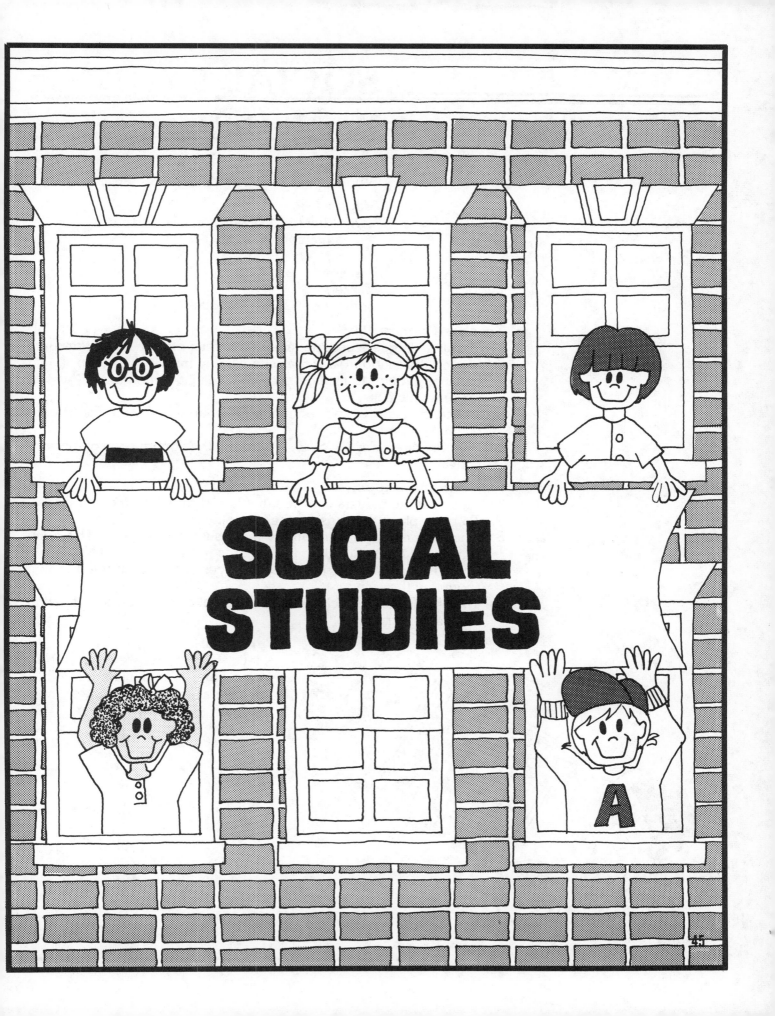

SOCIAL STUDIES

SOCIAL STUDIES
Map It Out

Purpose:
Students will read directions on a map.

Materials:
Large sheet of tagboard or rolled paper
Margarine container
Spinner
Fastener
Markers
Bottle caps (2 or 3, all different)

Teacher Preparation:
1. Using the large sheet of paper and markers, make a map of the area around the school. Place the school in the middle. The map should be large enough to include streets, buildings, and points of interest for several blocks.
2. Attach the fastener and spinner to the bottom of the margarine container.
3. Print the directions (N, S, E, W) around the bottom edge of the container.

Student Directions:
1. Two or three players choose a bottle cap to use as a game piece.
2. To start, place the caps on the school.
3. Choose a finishing point on the map, such as the park. (This point can be different each time the game is played.)
4. Each player spins the spinner and moves one block in the direction shown by the spinner.
5. The first player to reach the finishing point can select the destination for the next game.

Variation:
*Have the students prepare the map. They could build a three-dimensional map using boxes and scraps.

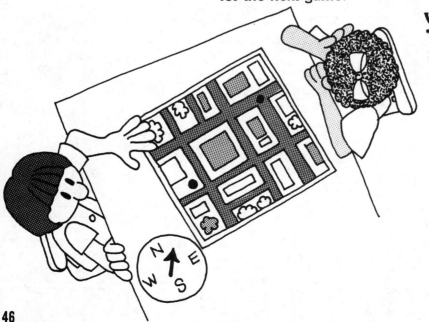

SOCIAL STUDIES

Travel Mobile

Purpose:
Students will display their research projects.

Materials:
Styrofoam meat trays
Markers
String or thin wire

Teacher Preparation:
Display the materials.

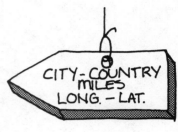

Student Directions:
1. Choose a city and country to research.
2. On one side of the tray, write the country, the city's latitude, longitude and distance in miles from your home.
3. On the other side of the tray, write the population, the main industry, the products, and the President's name.
4. Construct a mobile using the wire.

Variations:
*Use sweet roll containers instead of meat trays.

*Display other facts on the mobiles, such as famous people. Glue a picture to one side and write facts about the person on the other.

SOCIAL STUDIES
Original Origins

Purpose:
Students will read labels and find locations on a map.

Materials:
A large variety of containers
World map
Pushpins

Teacher Preparation:
1. Place the world map on a bulletin board.
2. Display the materials.

Student Directions:
1. Choose a container.
2. Read the label and locate the origin of the product.
3. Find the location on the map.
4. Use a pushpin to mark the location on the map.

Variations:
*Count the number of times each product name appears on its container. Graph the results or rank the order.

*Make a contents list for each product. Later have students match the lists with the containers.

*Have each student choose a container he or she likes. Research the origin of the food. Example: lemonade. Write a short report telling how and where lemons are grown and why they are useful to humans.

SOCIAL STUDIES

Zero In

Purpose:
Students will identify their planet, continent, country, state, county, and community.

Materials:
Pizza wheel
Pizza box
2 game pieces
1 die
Marker

Teacher Preparation:
1. Prepare the gameboard on the pizza wheel as shown in the diagram.
2. Store the gameboard, die, and game pieces in the pizza box.
3. Print the directions on the box.

Student Directions:
1. Two players each choose a game piece.
2. Start outside the circles.
3. Take turns rolling the die. The first player who rolls a 6, moves to the outer circle, names his or her planet (Earth), and takes another turn rolling the die. In order to move to the next circle, the player must roll a 5.
4. The game ends when a player moves to the center circle and names his or her community.

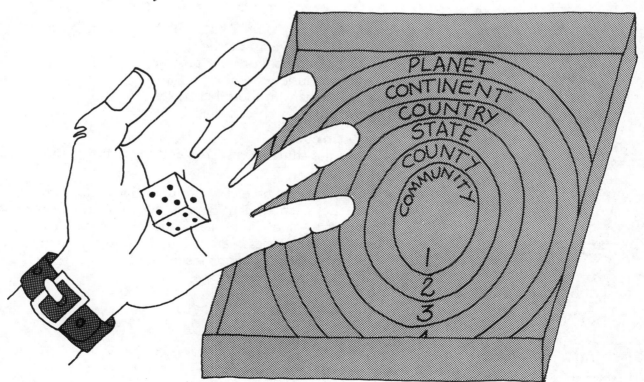

SOCIAL STUDIES

Heroes and Heroines of History

Purpose:
Students will arrange events in chronological order.

Materials:
Fast-food sandwich boxes
Construction paper
Scissors
Markers
Glue

Teacher Preparation:
1. Cut the paper into cards that fit inside the sandwich boxes.
2. On one card, glue a picture of a famous person. Glue the card to the outside lid of the sandwich box.
3. On a second card, print the person's name and event for which the person is famous.
   Example: Charles A. Lindbergh made the first nonstop airplane flight across the Atlantic Ocean.
4. Glue that card in the box on the left side.
5. On a third card, print the date of the event (1927).
6. Glue that card in the box on the right side.
7. Make several similar boxes.

1. Look at the picture on the lid of the box. Try to name the person. Tell the event and the date.
2. Open the box and check your answer.
3. Read the facts inside the box.
4. Repeat the steps with the other boxes.
5. Put all the boxes in chronological order.

Variations:
* Have the students research and make boxes for famous people.
* Have students predict the future. Give each student a box. Let each student draw a picture of a classmate or himself to glue on the lid. Students can predict an event that the classmate will be famous for, along with a date. Glue predictions inside the box.

SOCIAL STUDIES

A Capital Game

Purpose:
Students will review the state capitals.

Materials:
A large map of the United States, with only the states labeled
100 bottle caps (50 each of 2 colors)
Marker
Paper
2 margarine containers

Teacher Preparation:
1. Make a key by listing the state capitals on paper and assigning each a number.
2. Number each set of bottle caps 1-50.
3. Place a set of bottle caps in each margarine container.

Student Directions:
1. The map of the United States is a gameboard.
2. Each of two players gets a set of 50 bottle caps.
3. Players take turns drawing bottle caps and reading the numerals.
4. Look up the number in the key. Read the name of the city.
5. Decide which state the capital belongs in.
6. Place the bottle cap on the correct state on the map.
7. Continue playing until all the states are covered.

Variation:
*Provide a map with the states and capitals labeled so the children can check themselves.

SOCIAL STUDIES
Our Town

Purpose:
Students will study the areas of a community and build a model town.

Materials:
Variety of containers
Paint
Markers
Large sheet of rolled paper
Glue
Construction paper

Teacher Preparation:
1. Display the materials.
2. Divide the class into small groups or work as a whole class.

Student Directions:
1. Choose a container and design it as a house.
2. Spread the large sheet of paper on the floor. Draw streets for your town.
3. Divide the town into the following areas: commercial, industrial, recreational, and residential.
4. Place your house in a residential area of town.
5. Complete the town by designing buildings and other features for each area.

SOCIAL STUDIES

Job Jumble

Purpose:
Students will study various careers and match job requirements to jobs.

Materials:
5 or 6 shoe boxes
Construction paper
Cards
Markers

Teacher Preparation:
1. Use the paper and markers to label each box with a different job or career.
   Examples: teacher   computer operator   store manager
                  medical doctor   photographer   bus driver
                  lawyer   sales clerk   baseball umpire
                  architect   police officer   carpenter
                  airplane pilot   farmer   chef
                  fire fighter
2. Display the materials.
3. Divide the class into small groups.

Student Directions:
1. Think of several skills needed for each job. Print each skill on a different card.
   Examples: math ability   physical strength (or stamina)
                  creativity   manual dexterity
                  college degree   ability to organize details
                  advanced degree   liking to help other people
                  speaking ability   ability to get along with people
2. Sort the cards into the correct shoe boxes.

Variations:
*List the skills needed for each job.
*Compare lists with another group.
*Make a chart that shows all the skills needed for each job.

SOCIAL STUDIES
Puzzling Places

Purpose:
Students will study a map.

Materials:
Shoe box or oatmeal box
2 identical maps
Scissors

Teacher Preparation:
1. Cut one map into pieces to resemble a jigsaw puzzle.
2. Store the pieces in the container.
3. Display the other map.

Student Directions:
1. Pour out the puzzle pieces.
2. Put the pieces together to form a map. Use the map on display as a guide.

SOCIAL STUDIES

Shoe Box Celebrity

Purpose:
Students will research a famous person.

Materials:
Shoe box for each student
Construction paper
Markers
Glue
Scissors
Resource materials, such as encyclopedias, books,
magazines, newspapers, brochures

Teacher Preparation:
Display the materials.

Student Directions:
1. Choose a famous person, dead or alive, that you would like to study.
2. Decorate your shoe box with photographs or newspaper headlines about the person.
3. As you gather information about the person, put it in your box.
4. Help other students by sharing any information you may find about **their** famous people.
5. Report to the class what you have learned about the person.

Main Street

Purpose:
Students will research the architecture and equipment of industries that existed 100 years ago; they will build miniature models of the businesses.

Materials:
Cardboard containers of all sizes
Glue
Paint
Construction paper
Markers
Resource materials, such as encyclopedias, books, history magazines

Teacher Preparation:
1. Divide the class into small groups. Have each group choose an industry to study, such as a blacksmith shop, wagon shop, or gristmill.
2. Display the materials.

Student Directions:
1. Choose a business from 100 years ago.
2. Research the industry to find out its purpose, how it looked, and what equipment was needed to run the business.
3. Use the containers and other materials to build a miniature model of the business. Leave an opening so that you can show how the inside of the building looked.
4. Tell the class about your business.

Variation:
*Have the students hypothesize about the future and build miniature models of businesses they think will be needed.

SCIENCE

SCIENCE
Bag a Branch

Purpose:
Students will see evidence of plant transpiration.

Materials:
1 clear plastic bag without holes (8" x 12" or larger)
String, cord, or twist tie

Teacher Preparation:
1. Plan this project for a warm, sunny day in late spring, summer, or early fall.
2. Display the materials.
3. Divide students into small teams.

Students Directions:
1. Choose a deciduous tree on or near the school ground.
2. Slip the plastic bag over the end of a branch, enclosing as many leaves as possible.
3. Gather the open end of the bag tightly around the branch and tie with string or a twist tie.
4. Write down what you think will happen.
5. After several hours, check the bag.
6. How do the results compare with what you expected to happen?
7. Remove the bag from the branch.

Variations:
*Bag several branches and compare rates of transpiration. Weigh the bags before and after. Graph the results.
*Compare evergreens with deciduous trees.

SCIENCE

The Big Mix-Up

Purpose:
Students will study emulsion.

Materials:
Several clear soap containers with lids
A variety of substances, such as oil, water, food col-
oring, sand, soil, and milk
Resource materials
Paper
Pencils

Teacher Preparation:
1. Make a work sheet with questions for the children to explore
   and answer.
   Examples: Why do some pairs of substances not mix?
               Why do some pairs of substances stay mixed?
               What causes some mixtures to separate?
               If a mixture separates, what could you do to keep it
               mixed up?
2. Display the materials.

Student Directions:
1. Read the questions on the work sheet.
2. Mix several different pairs of substances in the containers.
3. Use your findings to answer the questions on the work sheet.
4. At the bottom of the work sheet, tell what the word *emulsion*
   means.

SCIENCE
Root View Box

Purpose:
Students will identify plant parts, observe plant development, and understand the factors necessary for plant growth.

Materials:
Half-gallon milk carton
3 sheets of Plexiglas, ¾″ x 8″
Soil (commercial mix or garden)
Seeds or bulbs (vegetable, herb, or flower)
Utility knife
Masking tape
Plastic wrap
Rubber band

Teacher Preparation:
1. Display the materials.
2. Observe as students prepare the box.

Student Directions:
1. Cut the top from a half-gallon milk carton.
2. Cut a flap from one side of the milk carton, leaving a ½″ border at the sides and bottom and a 1″ border along the top.
3. Tape the Plexiglas in the box at an angle from the front top to back bottom. (Roots follow gravity, so the angle helps ensure their visibility.)
4. Add premoistened soil.
5. Plant seeds ¼″ from the Plexiglas.
6. Cover the top with plastic wrap for faster sprouting. Fasten with the rubber band.
7. Keep the flap taped shut except at viewing times, since roots grow away from light.

Variations:
*Use this project to show how seeds sprout, how roots develop in various soil types, the effects of fertilizer, the regeneration of root cuttings, and water movement through the soil.
*Use bean seeds for fast sprouting or radish seeds for quick, interesting root development.

SCIENCE

Baby Jar Mystery

Purpose:
Students will make butter.

Materials:
½ pint of whipping cream or heavy cream
4 junior-sized baby food jars
Measuring cups

Teacher Preparation:
1. Display the materials.
2. Divide the class into four small groups.

Student Directions:
1. Measure 2 ounces (¼ cup) of whipping cream into the baby food jar.
2. Put the lid on *tightly*.
3. Take turns shaking the jar until the contents are solid.
4. Taste the results. Guess what it is.

Variation:
*Students may want to eat the butter on muffins or crackers.

SCIENCE
The Airless Plant

Purpose:
Students will attempt to grow plants in an environment without air.

Materials:
Transparent plastic container with lid
Utility knife
Plastic tape
Drinking straw
Potting soil
Water
Bean seeds

Teacher Preparation:
1. Cut a small "x" in the lid so that the straw can be inserted.
2. Display the materials.
3. Review with students the four elements necessary for plant growth: soil, light, air, and water. Tell students they will test whether plants can grow without air.

Student Directions:
1. Place a small amount of soil into the cup.
2. Plant two or three bean seeds in the soil.
3. Add a little bit of water.
4. Put the lid on the cup. Seal around the edge with plastic tape.
5. Insert a straw through the "x" in the lid. Do not let the straw touch the soil.
6. Seal the opening around the straw with plastic tape.
7. Have a volunteer "suck out" the air inside the cup through the straw, creating a vacuum.
8. Seal the top of the straw immediately with tape.
9. Chart any growth or changes observed.

Variations:
*To follow the scientific method of research, students may write the question, state their hypotheses, describe their procedures, chart or graph their findings, and record the results.

*Students may want to try growing a plant without light, without water, or without soil.

SCIENCE
Squeeze Me

Purpose:
Students will measure and compare hand strengths.

Materials:
Clear plastic squeeze bottle without lid
Permanent marker
Water

Teacher Preparation:
1. Mark a waterline 2" from the bottom of the bottle.
2. From the waterline, mark the bottle at ½" intervals. Number the marks from 1 to 10.
3. Fill with water to the waterline.

Student Directions:
1. Hold the bottle at the base in one hand, straight up.
2. Squeeze the bottle as hard as you can.
3. Record the highest level the water reaches.
4. Compare hand strengths with a partner or with the whole class.

Variation:
*Have students test the strengths of both their right and left hands and graph the results. From the graphs, can the class guess the dominant hand of each student?

SCIENCE
Under Pressure

Purpose:
Students will observe changes in air pressure.

Materials:
Coffee can
Large balloon
Rubber band
9" x 6" poster board
Small drinking straw
Tape
Marker
Resource materials
Commercial barometer

Teacher Preparation:
1. Cut the balloon to fit over the top of the coffee can.
2. Secure the balloon with a rubber band.
3. Cut one end of the straw to form a point.
4. Tape the other end of the straw to the balloon, pointed end to the side.
5. At the top of the poster board, print *barometer*.
6. Tape the poster board to the back of the can.
7. Above the straw pointer, print *high*. Below the pointer, print *low*.

Student Directions:
1. Observe any movement in the straw.
2. Find out what it means when the straw moves toward "high" or "low."
3. Compare the commercial barometer readings with the movement of the straw.

Variation:
*Have students construct the coffee can barometer.

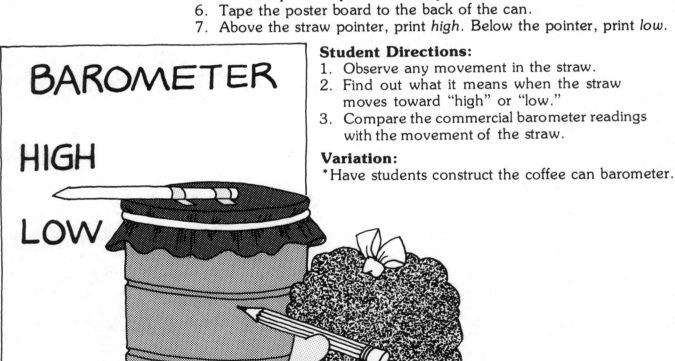

SCIENCE
Ear Model

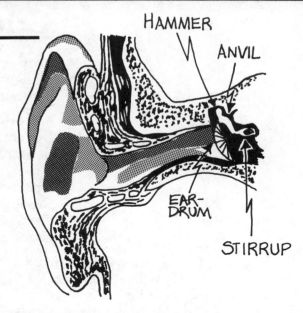

HAMMER
ANVIL
EAR-DRUM
STIRRUP

Purpose:
Students will build a model of an ear.

Materials:
Paper plate
Can
Tape
Wire
Thin paper
Resource materials
Scissors
Marker

Teacher Preparation:
Display the materials.

Student Directions:
1. Research the parts of an ear. Then follow the steps to build a model of an ear.
2. In the paper plate, cut a hole the same size as the can.
3. Insert the can in the hole.
4. Make the eardrum from the thin paper and tape it in place.
5. Make the hammer, anvil, and stirrup from the wire and tape them in place.
6. Label the parts.

SCIENCE
Cricket Cage

Purpose:
Students will find out whether crickets are reliable thermometers.

Materials:
Doughnut box or shoe box
Scissors
Tape
Nylon hose or netting
Resource materials
Thermometer
Clock or watch with a second hand

Teacher Preparation:
1. Plan this project for September, when crickets are plentiful and chirp a lot.
2. Display the materials.

Student Directions:
1. To make the cage, cut holes in the box.
2. Tape panels of nylon hose or netting over the holes. This will keep the cricket inside the cage and give it air.
3. Find out what crickets eat and provide the food.
4. Place a cricket in the cage and keep it in the classroom.
5. From time to time, figure the temperature by means of this formula: The number of chirps in 15 seconds + 40 = the temperature in degrees Fahrenheit.
6. Compare the cricket temperature with the temperature shown by the thermometer. Record both readings.
7. Take the cricket cage, the thermometer, and the watch outside. Test the formula in several places, checking your results with the thermometer.
8. Plot the pairs of readings on a graph. Is the cricket a reliable thermometer?

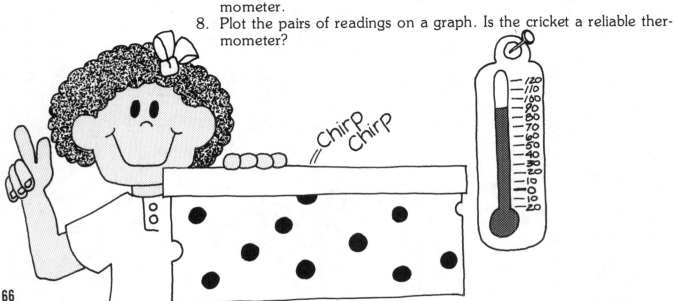

SCIENCE

Well Drilling

Purpose:
Students will observe how substances settle and simulate drilling wells.

Materials:
Clear liquid soap container
A variety of substances: soil, sand, bits of rock, coal, water
Drinking straw
Resource materials
Paper
Pencil

Teacher Preparation:
Display the materials.

Student Directions:
1. Layer the substances into the soap container.
2. Shake the container gently from side to side.
3. Write what you observe about how the substances settle.
4. Show how a well is drilled by "drilling" through the layers with a straw.
5. Write what you observed.
6. Research different types of wells. If you were to drill a well, what kind would it be—oil, gas, or water? What kinds of problems might you find? Write down your answer.

SCIENCE
You Are What You Eat

Purpose:
Students will categorize food into the four food groups.

Materials:
Two-sided fast-food sandwich container
Magazines and newspapers
Scissors
4, 3″ x 3″ sheets of paper
Marker
Glue
Paper
Pencils

Teacher Preparation:
1. On each sheet of paper, print a different food group.
   Milk and Milk Products
   Meat, Fish, Poultry, Nuts, and Legumes
   Fruits and Vegetables
   Breads, Cereals, and Grains
2. Glue the labels into the four sections of the sandwich container.
3. Display the materials.

Student Directions:
1. Cut pictures of food from the magazines and newspapers.
2. Place each picture in the correct food group container.
3. Could any food pictures be classified in more than one food group? Write on the paper why you think so.
4. A deluxe cheeseburger has mayonnaise, pickles, onions, catsup, mustard, tomatoes, and lettuce. Write the food groups that are included in this sandwich. List each ingredient under the correct food group.

Variations:
*Provide food containers, such as vegetable cans, fruit cans, tuna cans, cereal boxes, and nut cans. Have the students categorize the containers into food groups.
*Place pictures of food into "lunch boxes" made from doughnut boxes. Create appealing lunches using all of the food groups.

You Are What You Eat Example Page

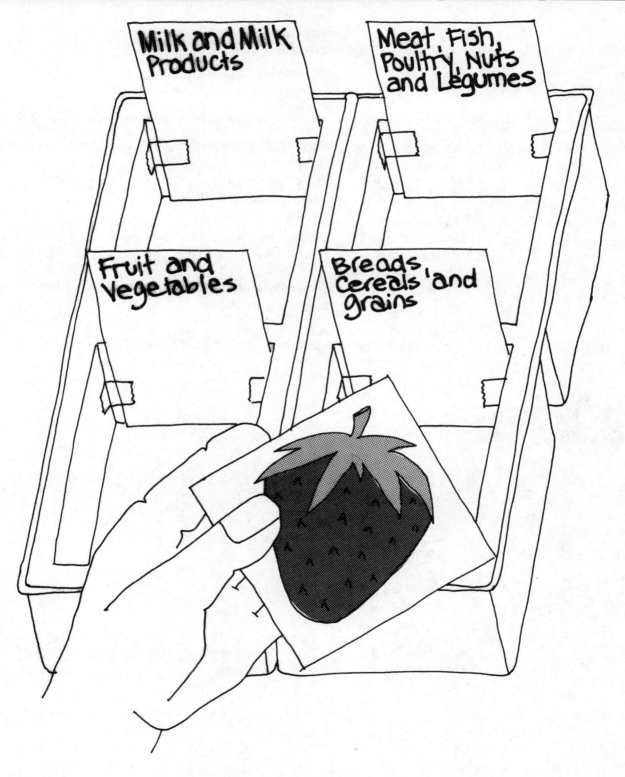

Science

Is It Alive?

Purpose:
Students will sort items into living and nonliving categories.

Materials:
2 margarine tubs for each student
Markers

Teacher Preparation:
1. Plan a walk or field trip to a site where the students can gather various small objects.
2. Introduce the concept of living and nonliving to the students.
3. Give each student two margarine tubs.

Student Directions:
1. Label one tub "Living" and the other "Nonliving."
2. On your walk, gather items and place them in the appropriate margarine tubs.
3. After you return, share the items with the class. Tell why each item belongs in the category you chose.

Variation:
*Have the children cut out or draw pictures of objects to place in the appropriate containers.

SCIENCE

Body Systems

Purpose:
Students will review the parts and systems of the body.

Materials:
1 large envelope
Several small envelopes
Game cards
Markers

Teacher Preparation:
1. Label the large envelope "Body Systems."
2. Print the student directions on the large envelope.
3. On each small envelope, write the name of a body system.
   (Examples: circulatory, skeletal, muscular, nervous, digestive)
4. Print the name of a body part on each game card.
   (Examples: stomach, brain, femur, spinal cord, biceps)
5. Store all of the pieces in the large envelope.

Student Directions:
1. Read the game cards.
2. Match each card to the correct body system. Place the card in the envelope where it belongs.

Variations:
*Draw or glue pictures of body parts on some of the cards
*Have the students prepare the game cards as they study each body system.

SCIENCE
Chicks Pix

Purpose:
Students will study the stages of chicken embryology.

Materials:
Egg-shaped panty hose containers
Small pieces of paper
Markers
Resource materials

Teacher Preparation:
Display the materials.

Student Directions:
1. Research the stages of a chicken embryo's development.
2. On the small pieces of paper, draw pictures of the developing embryo.
3. Place a drawing inside each egg container.
4. Open the eggs and tell how old each embryo is.
5. Arrange the eggs in the correct order.

Variation:
*Copy the patterns of the chicken embryo stages on the next page to place inside the egg containers.

SCIENCE
Chicks Pix Pictures

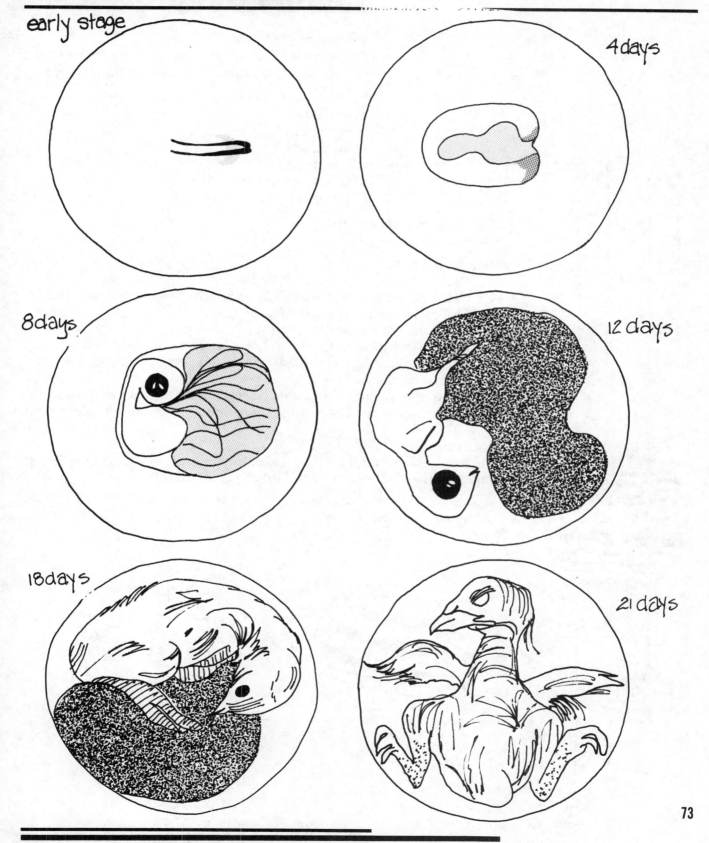

early stage

4 days

8 days

12 days

18 days

21 days

SCIENCE
Ceiling Solar System

Purpose:
Students will research the names and relative sizes of the planets and understand the spatial relationships in the solar system.

Materials:
9 pizza wheels
Hole punch
White thread
Markers or tempera paint
Paper clip hangers or tape

Teacher Preparation:
Display the materials.

Student Directions:
1. Research the planets and their sizes.
2. Use pizza wheels that are the same relative sizes as the nine planets. The scale can be approximate or exact.
3. Cut a ring of a circle to go around Saturn.
4. Design and label the planets, using markers or paint.
5. Show the location and giant size of the sun by marking part of its outline on the wall.
6. Hang the planets from the ceiling, using the white thread and hangers or tape. Use your research data as a guide to placement.

Variations:
*Instead of labeling the planets with their names, write several descriptive sentences that end with "What planet am I?"
*For a more three-dimensional effect, two pizza wheels could be slotted together for each planet.

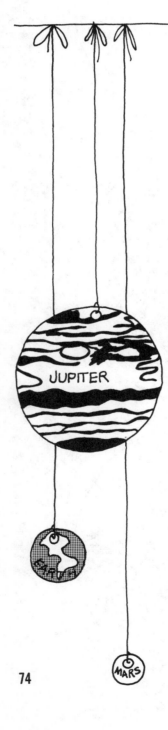

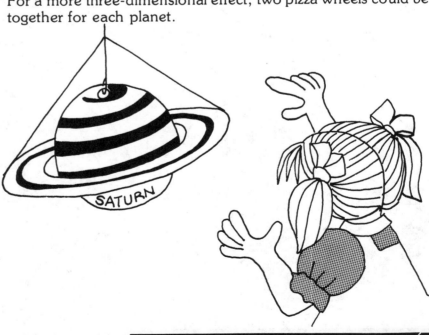

BULLETIN BOARD

Spacey History

Purpose:
Students will research the history of space exploration and travel, develop vocabulary and writing skills, and display the information.

Materials:
Colored yarn
15-20 large fast-food French fry boxes
French fry and prize patterns
Construction paper
Pins or stapler
Pencils
Markers
Large bulletin board for display
Resource materials

Teacher Preparation:
1. Display the materials.
2. Supervise the preparation of the bulletin board.

Student Directions:
1. Gather information about space exploration from the resource materials. List all the dates and events.
2. Cut or draw letters to make the title, "Spacey History." Pin or staple the title at the top of the bulletin board.
3. Make a time line on the bulletin board. Pin or staple a long piece of colored yarn across the board.
4. Beginning at the left, staple the French fry boxes along the line to mark every two years.
5. Label the year on each box. Begin with the year of the earliest space exploration event you found.
6. Under the time line, pin or staple four children's meal boxes. Label these boxes:
   Satellites
   Space Vehicles
   Astronauts
   World Changes Due to Space Exploration
7. Write each date and event you found on a French fry cut from construction paper.
8. Place the events in the correct fry containers along the time line.
9. Write information about satellites, space vehicles, astronauts, and world changes on "prizes" cut from construction paper.
10. Place each prize in the correct child's meal box.

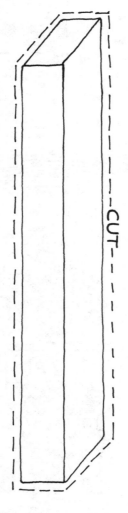

CUT

BULLETIN BOARD

Spacey History Bulletin Board

Spacey History Pattern Page

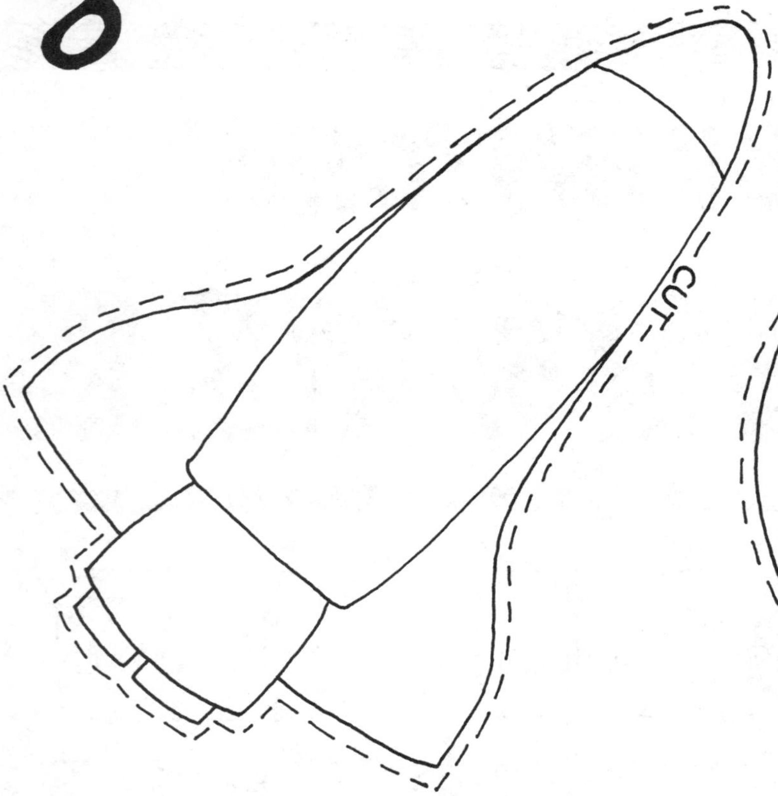

CUT

CUT

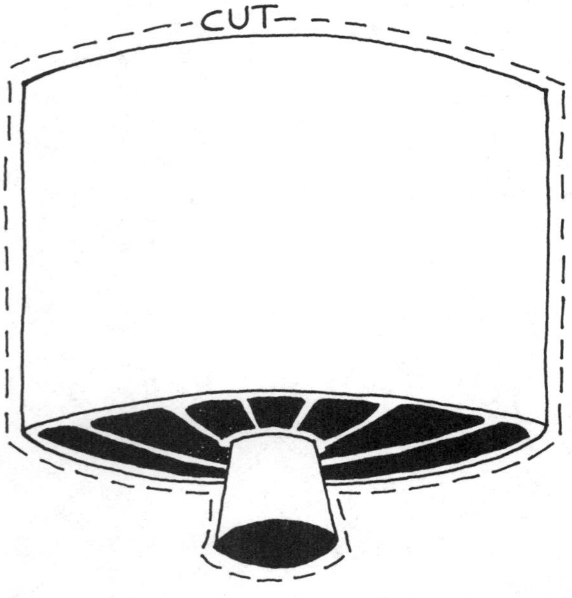

CUT

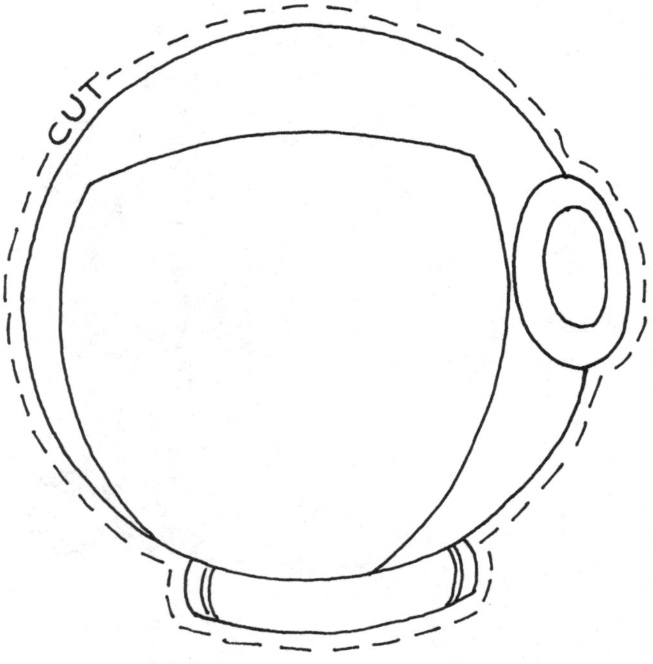

CUT

BULLETIN BOARD

From Trees to Containers

Purpose:
Students will gather a variety of containers that are made from trees.

Materials:
Construction paper
Scissors
Stapler

Teacher Preparation:
1. From construction paper, cut letters for the title, "From Trees to Containers."
2. Staple the title at the top of the bulletin board.
3. Construct on the board a large paper tree that has many branches and leaves.

Student Directions:
1. Collect containers that are made from trees, such as envelopes, sacks, pizza wheels, and cardboard boxes.
2. Staple each container to a tree branch on the bulletin board.

Variation:
*Have students collect containers that are made from oil, coal, or metal.

BULLETIN BOARD
Flip Your Lid

Purpose:
This activity is designed to reinforce quick recall of basic social studies facts.

Materials:
20 opaque fast-food sandwich containers
Markers
Timer (optional)
Construction paper

Teacher Preparation:
1. Title a bulletin board "Flip Your Lid."
2. Develop questions and answers in four or five categories.
   Examples:

Famous People	Famous Places
Capitals/States	Current Events

3. Print the categories on construction paper and place them horizontally across the bulletin board under the title.
4. Assign each question a point value based on its difficulty in the category.
   Examples: 10, 20, 30, 40, 50
5. Write the answer to each question on the outside of a sandwich container. Write the question inside the container.
   Example: Outside—The man who invented the telephone
   Inside—Who was Alexander Graham Bell?
6. Place the containers and the point values vertically under each category, least difficult to most difficult.

Student Directions:
1. Three students may play the game at one time. The moderator keeps score and reads the answers.
2. Set a time limit for the game.
3. The moderator reads the answer on a container. The contestant must give the correct question. If the contestant is correct, the moderator flips the lid down, revealing the question.
4. A contestant's turn continues as long as he or she replies accurately.
5. At the end of the set time, points are totaled for each player.

Variations:
*Students can help develop more questions and answers to keep the game new.
*Play the same game with different subjects, such as math, science, or literature.

BULLETIN
BOARD

Flip Your Lid Bulletin Board

FLIP YOUR LID

FAMOUS PEOPLE	CAPITALS/ STATES	FAMOUS PLACES	CURRENT EVENTS
10	10	10	10
20	20	20	20
30	30	30	30

BULLETIN BOARD

Let's Face It

Purpose:
Students will reinforce basic multiplication facts.

Materials:
24 plain paper plates
Scissors
Stapler
Markers
Construction paper
16 spring clothespins
Glue

Teacher Preparation:
1. Cut eight of the paper plates in half.
2. Staple each half to a whole plate. You will have sixteen plate faces.
3. Cut eyes for the faces. Glue two to each plate half.
4. Cut large smiles and glue one onto each face.
5. Print a multiplication fact on each smile.
6. Cut noses for the faces and glue one to each clothespin.
7. Print the answer to a fact on each nose.
8. Display the faces on a bulletin board.

Student Directions:
1. Match the answers on the noses to the facts on the smiles.
2. Clip the correct nose onto each face.
3. Have a friend check your answers.

Variations:
*Have the students make the faces.
*Design the faces as jack-o'-lanterns, cats, or other seasonal objects or animals.
*Use this activity to match any kind of facts.
*Prepare an answer key for self-checking.

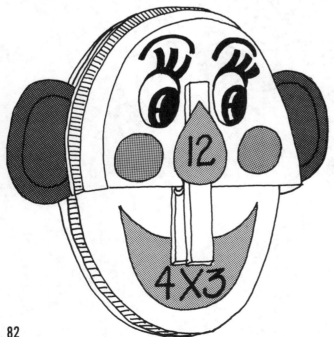

BULLETIN
BOARD

Let's Face It Bulletin Board

BULLETIN BOARD

Guess the Guest

Purpose:
Students will recall famous people.

Materials:
Fast-food sandwich containers
Construction paper
Marker
Pushpins
2 shoe boxes
1 envelope
Large bulletin board
Scissors
Glue

Teacher Preparation:
1. Cut the sandwich containers in half.
2. Cut small pieces of construction paper to fit inside the containers.
3. Print a letter of the alphabet on each piece of paper. Glue a letter inside each container. Make several of each letter.
4. File the containers in alphabetical order in the shoe boxes.
5. Label the envelope "Famous People."
6. Cut small pieces of construction paper to fit inside the envelope.
7. Make category cards by writing the name of a famous person on each paper. Store the cards in the envelope.
8. Display the materials by a bulletin board.

Student Directions:
1. One person, playing the role of moderator, chooses a category card and finds the correct letters.
2. The moderator pins the letters on the bulletin board in the correct order, with the letters facing the board.
3. The players take turns guessing letters of the alphabet.
4. If a player guesses a hidden letter, the moderator turns the letter around so that it shows. The player gets another turn.
5. A player who guesses a letter correctly may also guess what the category card says.
6. The first player to correctly guess the category card answer wins the game and becomes the next moderator.
7. Each moderator must put the letters back in the shoe boxes in alphabetical order.

Variations:
*Have the students prepare the game materials.
*Make other category cards: animals, states, phrases, occupations, school subjects, parts of speech, vocabulary words, or holidays.

BULLETIN BOARD

Guess the Guest Bulletin Board

GUESS THE GUEST

FAMOUS PEOPLE

A □ E

□ LIN□OLN

BULLETIN BOARD
Design a Casserole

Purpose:
Students will learn what a casserole is, study the components of a recipe, and create and draw an original recipe.

Materials:
Construction paper
Scissors
Staplers
Tape
Grocery bags
Food containers (rice box, tuna can, meat tray, soup box, macaroni bag, spice containers, cheese package, etc.)
Recipe cards
Pencils
Drawing paper
Markers

Teacher Preparation:
1. From construction paper, cut the letters for the title, "Design a Casserole."
2. Print the definitions of the word *casserole* on construction paper. Casserole: 1) an earthenware or glass baking dish, usually with a cover, in which food can be cooked and then served. 2) the food baked and served in such a dish, usually rice, potatoes, or macaroni with meat or fish and vegetables.
3. Staple the title and the definitions to the bulletin board.
4. Staple or tape several grocery bags, along with the food containers, to the board.
5. Leave room for student drawings at the sides of the bulletin board.

Student Directions:
1. Read the definitions of the word *casserole*.
2. Create a recipe for a casserole. Use at least three of the ingredients shown on the bulletin board and add some of your own, if you want. Be sure your recipe has a list of ingredients, with amounts to use, and mixing and baking instructions.
3. Write your recipe on a recipe card.
4. Use drawing paper and markers to make a picture of your casserole.
5. Staple the drawing on the bulletin board.

Variations:
*Have students vote for their favorite casserole and graph the results.

*Arrange for students to interview the school cook.

*Ask a parent to come to school to demonstrate how a casserole is prepared. Serve the casserole for lunch.

BULLETIN BOARD

Design a Casserole Bulletin Board

DESIGN A CASSEROLE

casserole:
1. an earthenware or glass baking dish, usually with a cover, in which food can be cooked and then served.
2. the food baked and served in such a dish, usually rice, potatoes or macaroni with meat or fish and vegetables.

RICE

CHEESE

TUNA

Soup

Milk

ORE

BASIL

MACAR

16oz.

TASHA

BULLETIN BOARD

Stately Products

Purpose:
Students will find out what products come from their state.

Materials:
Construction paper
Scissors
Stapler
State map
Yarn
Pushpins
Resource materials
Paper
Pencils

Teacher Preparation:
1. Cut letters for a bulletin board title that includes the name of your state.
2. Staple the title to the bulletin board.
3. Staple a large state map to the center of the bulletin board.

Student Directions:
1. Pretend that the borders of your state are closed. You must rely on the products that come from your own state.
2. Find out what your state produces. Collect empty containers and pictures of those products.
3. Staple the containers and pictures on the bulletin board beside the map.
4. Use yarn and pushpins to connect each picture and container to the place on the map where the item is produced.
5. Make a list of products you would no longer be able to have.
6. Divide your state's food products into the four basic food groups. List the foods from each food group that you would not be able to get.

Variations:
*Have students research the products of several states. Which state would be the most self-sufficient? Which would be the least self-sufficient?

*Visit a local industry. Find out if all of the products used in the manufacturing process came from your state.

BULLETIN BOARD

Stately Products Bulletin Board

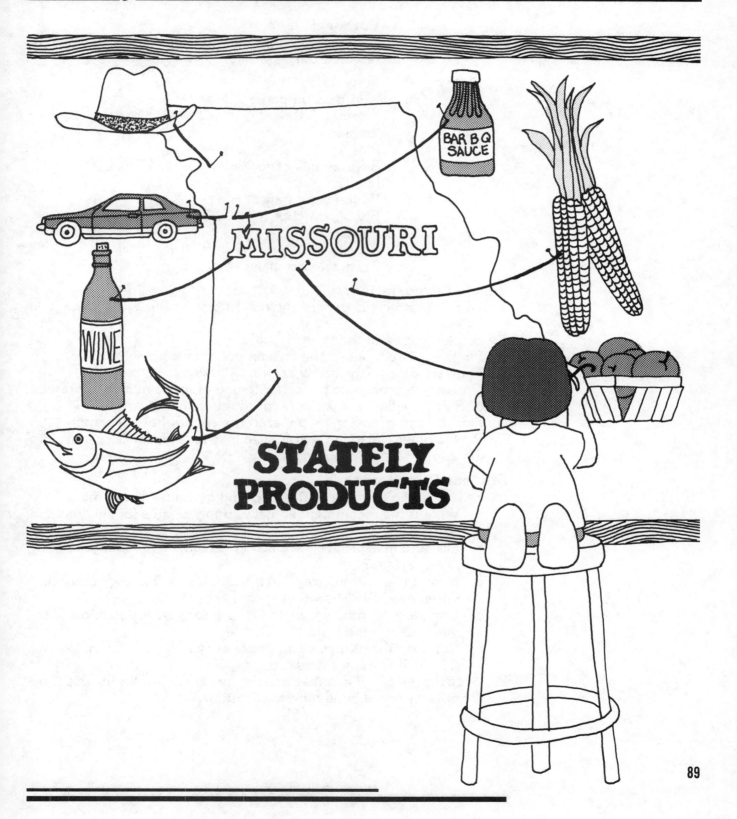

BULLETIN BOARD

What's in Milk?

Purpose:
Students will study the nutritional value of milk and research other questions about milk.

Materials:
Construction paper
Scissors
Stapler
Pins
Several milk cartons
Marker
White crepe paper
Styrofoam cups
Paper
Pencils
Resource materials

Teacher Preparation:
1. From construction paper, cut the letters for the title, "What's in Milk?"
2. Staple the title to the bulletin board.
3. Pin the milk cartons to the bulletin board in pouring position.
4. Pin a styrofoam cup below each milk carton.
5. On each strip of crepe paper, write one of milk's nutrients: protein, calcium, riboflavin, vitamin D, phosphorus.
6. Pin one end of the crepe paper to the spout of a milk carton.
7. Pin the other end to the styrofoam cup to resemble milk pouring into the cup.

Student Directions:
1. Research two or more of the following questions about milk:
   a. What is the recommended daily supply of milk for children and adults?
   b. Milk and milk products are rich in calcium. Why does your body need calcium?
   c. Most milk cartons say that the milk is *homogenized* and *pasteurized*. What do these terms mean?
   d. Compare the nutrients in whole milk to those found in baby formula. Graph the results.
   e. Compare the nutrients and calories in whole milk, 2% milk, and skim milk. Graph the results.
2. Write the results of your research on the paper. Display the paper on the bulletin board beside the milk cartons.

BULLETIN BOARD

What's in Milk? Bulletin Board

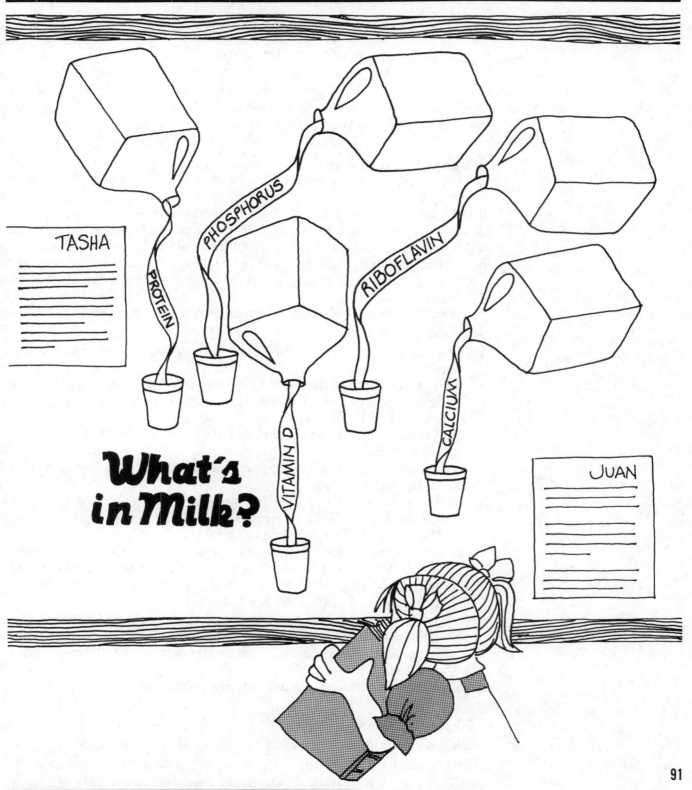

BULLETIN BOARD
Fast-Food Family

Purpose:
Students will study trash disposal and research related questions.

Materials:
Trash from one fast-food meal for a family of four
Resource materials   Poster board
Construction paper   Markers
Scissors   Stapler

Teacher Preparation:
1. From construction paper, cut letters for the title, "Fast-Food Family."
2. Staple the title at the top of the bulletin board.
3. Draw a picture of a family of four on the poster board and cut it out.
4. Staple the family to the middle of the bulletin board.
5. Collect the trash from one meal at a fast-food restaurant for a family of four: sandwich containers, napkins, French fry containers, and cups.
6. Staple the trash around the family on the bulletin board.

Student Directions:
1. Choose two or more of the following questions about trash to research:
   a. How do families dispose of their trash? Where does it go after the trash truck picks it up? How much trash does an average family dispose of each year?
   b. What is the rate of deterioration of paper, plastic, styrofoam, and metal cans?
   c. Define *ecology* and *biodegradable*. How are these words related to the study of trash?
   d. What are some ways to dispose of trash? Which do you think is the best way? What responsibilities do citizens have to see that their trash is disposed of properly?
   e. Packaging includes concerns about health, cost and convenience. Why don't fast-food restaurants use washable plates and metal utensils? Why do many places use styrofoam, instead of wax paper to wrap their sandwiches?
   f. What percentage of your fast-food dollar goes for packaging?
   g. How does the fast-food industry dispose of its trash? What problems with trash do restaurants have that are different from families?
2. Report to the class the results of your research.

Variations:
*Take a field trip to a landfill.
*Ask the manager of a fast-food restaurant to visit the class.
*Have students make posters, encouraging people to dispose of their trash properly, for the school cafeteria or local restaurants.

BULLETIN BOARD

Fast-Food Family Bulletin Board

BULLETIN BOARD

Definition Cartons

Purpose:
Students will use dictionary skills and study words that have multiple definitions.

Materials:
1 egg carton for each child
Construction paper
Stapler
Scissors
Dictionaries
Markers
Pencils
Glue

Teacher Preparation:
1. From construction paper, cut letters for the title, "Definition Cartons."
2. Staple the title to the bulletin board.
3. Give each student an egg carton.
4. Display the materials.

Student Directions:
1. Find a word in the dictionary that has many definitions, such as *sail* or *set*.
2. Use a marker to print the word on the inside of the egg carton lid.
3. Cut several small pieces of construction paper that will fit inside the egg cups.
4. On each piece of paper, print one definition for the word.
5. Glue a definition inside each egg cup.
6. Staple your egg carton onto the bulletin board.

CLASSROOM MANAGEMENT

CLASSROOM MANAGEMENT
Destination Pockets

Purpose:
The teacher will know at a glance where each student is.

Materials:
Several library card pockets
One index card for each student
Tape
Marker
Shoe box

Teacher Preparation:
1. On each library card pocket, print the name of a place a student might be going when he or she leaves the classroom: "Girls' Restroom," "Library," "Office," etc.
2. If a student goes to a special class, such as a remedial reading class, print the name of the teacher on the pocket.
3. If five students may go to the library at one time, prepare five pockets marked "Library."
4. Tape the pockets to a wall near the door.
5. Print the name of each student across the top of an index card, so that it can be read easily when it is in a pocket.
6. Place the students' cards into the shoe box near the door.

Student Directions:
1. Before you leave the classroom, find your index card in the shoe box.
2. Place your card in the pocket that tells where you are going. Be sure your name is showing.
3. When you return to the classroom, take your card out of the pocket and put it back in the shoe box.

Variation:
*For sturdier pockets, cover Band-Aid or French fry boxes.

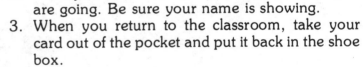

CLASSROOM MANAGEMENT

Slices of Jobs

Purpose:
Students will be able to see if they have a classroom job.

Materials:
Large pizza box
Pizza wheel
Tempera paints and brushes
Construction paper
Scissors
Glue
Markers
Pushpins

Teacher Preparation:
1. Attach the opened pizza box to a wall or bulletin board.
2. Paint a pizza on the pizza wheel.
3. Use a marker to divide the pizza into slices, one slice for each classroom job.
4. Label each slice with a job, such as line leader, recess equipment person, or door holder.
5. Glue the pizza in the pizza box.
6. Cut the construction paper into small squares.
7. Print the name of a student onto each square.
8. Pin one name onto each slice of pizza.
9. Pin the rest of the names to the lid of the pizza box.
10. Change the names on the slices daily or weekly.

Student Directions:
Check the pizza each day to find out if you have a classroom job for the day.

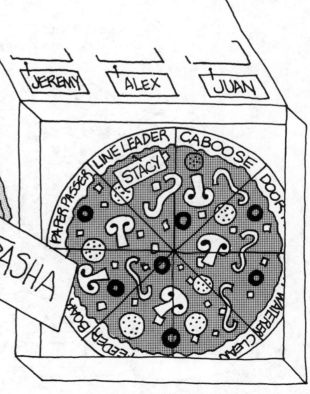

CLASSROOM MANAGEMENT
First-Aid Pals

Purpose:
Students will gather assignments and notes for a student who is absent.

Materials:
Detergent box
Scissors
White and red paper
Tape or glue

Teacher Preparation:
1. Cut the front cover from the detergent box.
2. Wrap the box in white paper.
3. Cut out four red crosses and glue one to each side of the box.
4. Divide the class into groups of three.

Student Directions:
1. When a student is absent from your group of three, the other two students are responsible for the red cross box. You will be the "first-aid pals."
2. Place the box on the desk of the absent student.
3. During the day, collect all assignments, notes, and work sheets for the student. Place them in the box.

Variation:
*Make arm bands with red crosses for the first-aid pals. This will identify them and remind them of their responsibility.

CLASSROOM MANAGEMENT

Who Goes Where?

Purpose:
Groups of students will be able to rotate to various learning centers with the help of a chart.

Materials:
Construction paper
Scissors
Pizza wheel
Glue
Marker
Poster board
Large brad

Teacher Preparation:
1. Divide the class into small groups. Assign each group of students a different color.
2. Divide the pizza wheel into as many sections as there are groups.
3. Cut a wedge of construction paper to fit each pizza wheel section. Use the colors assigned to the groups.
4. Glue the wedges onto the pizza wheel.
5. Center the pizza wheel on the poster board and attach it with the brad.
6. Around the wheel, print the names of the learning centers onto poster board.
7. Turn the wheel to show each group which center to use.

Student Directions:
1. Find your group's color on the pizza wheel.
2. Go to the learning center shown next to that color.

CLASSROOM MANAGEMENT
Teacher's Closet

Purpose:
Teachers will be able to organize and store materials in their closets.

Materials:
Shoe boxes
Hanging shoe storage container
Glue
Pegboard and hooks
Detergent boxes
Laundry bags or baskets
Containers in a variety of sizes

Teacher Preparation:
1. Use shoe boxes to store bulletin board letters. Have a different box for each color. Glue a sample letter to the outside of the box. Store the shoe boxes in a shoe storage container that is hung on the wall.
2. Use pegboards and hooks to hang coats, bags, and equipment. For large games, posters, maps, and bulletin board characters, punch two holes in the material and hang on two hooks on the pegboard.
3. Store math, science, art, and other materials in large, paper-covered detergent boxes.
4. Recess balls, jump ropes, and paint smocks can be stored in large laundry bags or baskets.

Student Directions:
Go into the teacher's closet only with permission.

CLASSROOM MANAGEMENT
Teacher's Closet Example Page

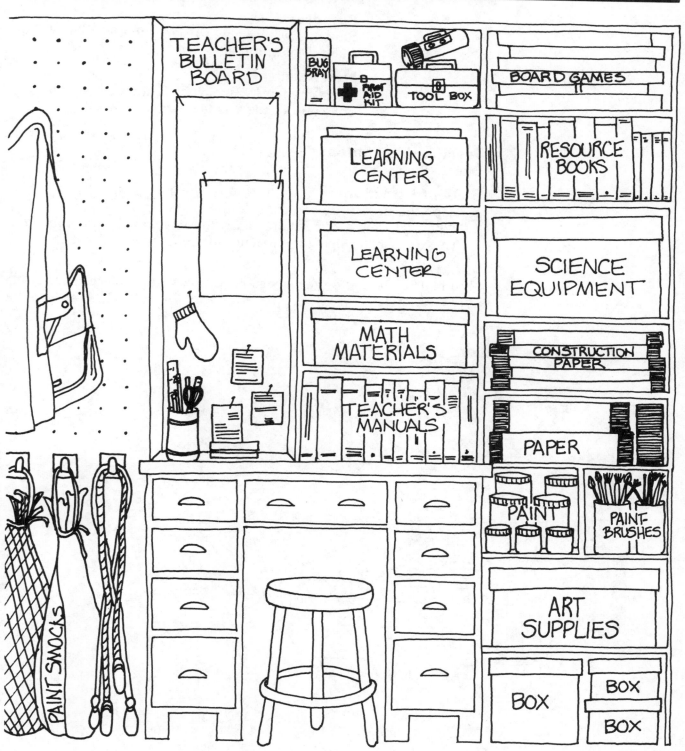

TEACHER'S BULLETIN BOARD

BUG SPRAY

FIRST AID KIT

TOOL BOX

BOARD GAMES

LEARNING CENTER

RESOURCE BOOKS

LEARNING CENTER

SCIENCE EQUIPMENT

MATH MATERIALS

CONSTRUCTION PAPER

TEACHER'S MANUALS

PAPER

PAINT

PAINT BRUSHES

ART SUPPLIES

PAINT SMOCKS

BOX

BOX

BOX

CLASSROOM MANAGEMENT

Silent Signal

Purpose:
Students will be able to signal the teacher for help without interrupting.

Materials:
Large French fry container (1 for each student)
Envelope (1 for each student)
Tape

Teacher Preparation:
Display the materials.

Student Directions:
1. Tape the French fry container to the side of your desk.
2. When you have a question, place the envelope in the container. This will silently signal the teacher that you have a question.

Variation:
* Students could write their questions on paper and place them inside the envelopes.

CLASSROOM MANAGEMENT

Job Jackets

Purpose:
Students will be able to organize classroom jobs.

Materials:
Large French fry container (1 for each job)
Large stickers
Note cards

Teacher Preparation:
1. Print the name of each job on a sticker.
2. Place the sticker over the fry symbol.
3. Arrange the fry containers on a bulletin board.

Student Directions:
1. For each job, print your name at the top of a note card.
2. Decorate your note cards.
3. Place one of your cards inside each fry container so that the name can be read.
4. Rotate the job assignments by moving the front names to the back as the jobs are completed.

CLASSROOM MANAGEMENT

Play It Safe

Purpose:
Students will use classroom and school safety rules to make a School Safety Zone.

Materials:
A variety of containers
Construction paper
Markers
Scissors
Glue

Teacher Preparation:
1. Lead the class in establishing classroom rules. Review school safety rules with students.
2. Display the materials.

Student Directions:
1. Decide what signs and markings are needed to keep the area in and around the school safe for students and others.
2. Use the containers and other materials to make safety signs.
   Examples: Stop
   Crosswalk
   No Smoking
   Walk in Hallways
   Keep Door Closed
3. Put up the signs.

Variations:
*Use the signs as visual aids in making a safety presentation to the school.
*Design similar signs for a Home Safety Zone. Determine the similarities and differences between school and home safety.

CLASSROOM MANAGEMENT

Package Deal

Purpose:
Students will make a message center for corresponding with each other and with the teacher.

Materials:
Round oatmeal boxes (1 for each person)
Paint
Glue
Small stickers

Teacher Preparation:
1. Give each student an oatmeal box.
2. Display the materials.

Student Directions:
1. Paint your oatmeal box.
2. Print your name on the sticker and place it just inside the edge, facing out.
3. Glue your box together with those of the other students, as shown in the diagram.
4. Be sure your name sticker can be read.

Variations:
*Use the boxes to hand out papers, missing assignments, or notes to take home.
*The teacher should have a mailbox, as well, for notes from students.
*Use the boxes to help students practice letter-writing skills. Have each student write a letter to another person in the class. Students can mail their letters and respond to letters they receive.

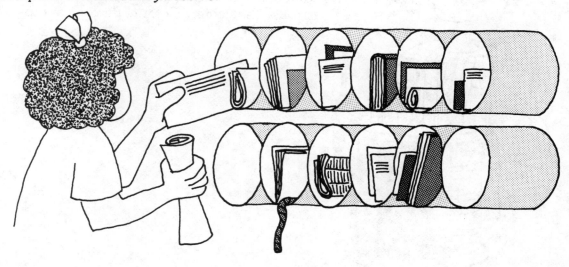

CLASSROOM MANAGEMENT

Coffee Can Management

Purpose:
Students will be able to take attendance each day.

Materials:
Large coffee can
Spring clothespins (1 for each student)
Con-Tact paper
Marker

Teacher Preparation:
1. Write the name of each child on a clothespin.
2. Cover the coffee can with Con-Tact paper.
3. Print the student directions on the can.
4. Clip the clothespins around the edge of the coffee can, name side out.

Student Directions:
1. When you come into the classroom each morning, take your clothespin from the outside of the can and drop it inside.
2. After everyone is seated, check the coffee can. The remaining clothespins should show those students who are absent.

Variations:
*This system can also help count hot lunch and milk buyers if you add two more cans of different colors.
*Manage learning center traffic by placing a coffee can in each area. The number of clothespins on the can indicates the number of students who can use the center. Color-code cans and pins for nonreaders.